CHANGE YOUR CULTURE, CHANGE YOUR WORLD

Companion to Understanding Kingdom Culture

Apostles Timothy and Pamela Williams

Change Your Culture Change Your World
Companion to Understanding Kingdom Culture

Books may be ordered through booksellers or by contacting:

Touch N Lives Around The World, LLC.

New Orleans LA 70174

Cr8ed2worship@sbcglobal.net

(504) 812-6809

www.touchnlives.com

ISBN-13: 987-0-615-42400-2

Library of Congress Number: 2013932226

All Scripture quotations, unless otherwise noted, are taken from the King James Version of the Bible.

TABLE OF CONTENTS

"YOU MUST BE THE CHANGE

YOU WISH TO SEE IN THE WORLD."

MAHATMA GHANDI

ACKNOWLEDGEMENTS

In all thy ways ***acknowledge him****, and he shall direct thy paths.*

Proverbs 3:6

To the Triune God; the three in one; God the Father, Jesus Christ the Son and the Holy Spirit. We acknowledge you and thank you for your prompting, leading and guidance.

To the wife of my youth: best friend and co-laborer in the ministry. On behalf of our children, grandchildren and I, we would like to thank you for all you do and have done to bring completeness to our lives. We can truly say that you are, A Proverbs 31 woman. May God bless and keep you.

For though ye have ten thousand instructors in Christ, yet have ye ***not many fathers****: for in Christ Jesus I have begotten you through the gospel.*

1 Corinthians 4:15

DEDICATION

A good man leaveth an inheritance to his children's children: and the wealth of the sinner is laid up for the just. **Proverbs 13:22**

To all of our children and their children, this is for you. Thank you for your love and support. May God bless you all.

PREFACE

It was in 1963 when the Late Great Sam Cooke penned and first recorded the song: "A Change Is Gonna Come," which was released shortly after his death in 1964 by RCA Victor label. At that time the song was a modest hit compared to some of his previous singles. It later came to exemplify the sixties' Civil Rights Movement and gained popularity and critical acclaim in the later decades. This song is still touching lives today and is number twelve on the Rolling Stone's 500 greatest songs of All Time list.

When I think about this song and the message behind it, I think about a sermon I heard Apostle Vincent G. Valentyn preach about the Kingdom of God at a prayer breakfast. He said, "Until there is a model in the earth, God will keep being persistent." The message here is this: God is looking for a model in the earth to exemplify the model in heaven. Until He finds that model, He will continue to look. This is what Jesus was referring to when He taught His disciples to pray.

He told them in Luke 11:2 "When ye pray, say, Our Father which art in heaven, Hallowed be thy name, Thy kingdom come. Thy will be done, as in heaven, so in earth…." I like the way it is said in Matthew 6:10 "Thy kingdom come. Thy will be done in earth, as it is in heaven." (KJV)

God is seeking culture change. Why, you may ask? Culture is like second nature. It is a part of you. It identifies who you are, what you believe and where you are from. Some say all you need is to understand Kingdom Precepts, while others say, what you need is Kingdom Consciousness.

We say, both of these concepts are great but they require work, memory and practice, whereas culture is a part of you, your heritage and who you represent.

God wants to see change in our lives especially if we are going in a direction that pulls us away from Him. He would rather see us change than see us destroyed. 2 Peter 3:9 says, "God is not willing that any should perish but that all should come to repentance." We often talk about how and why God destroyed Sodom and Gomorrah. There are several other instances where God destroyed cities, villages and scores of people.

Nineveh was a city God sent warning to. God told Jonah that He was going to destroy Nineveh. He took Jonah through great troubles to get him to go and preach in Nineveh.

In the end, Jonah was very displeased with God because of the many trials and tribulations he went through before deciding to obey God and go preach in Nineveh. Jonah was angry because God did not destroy Nineveh as He said He would. Jonah just could not understand this. What Jonah didn't realize was, as far as God was concerned, the mission was accomplished. The objective was to get the people of Nineveh to repent. After Jonah preached to Nineveh, the people repented, changed their ways and turned to the Lord, therefore there was no need for God to destroy Nineveh because the objective was achieved.

Let's take a look at how this change came about. After the preaching of Jonah, the people of Nineveh believed God. They proclaimed a fast and put on sackcloth, from the greatest of them to the least of them. When the king of Nineveh heard word of this, he arose from his throne, took off his robe and covered himself with sackcloth and sat in ashes. The king and all his nobles made a decree and had it published throughout Nineveh that said, "Let neither man nor beast, herd nor flock taste anything; let them not feed nor drink water; but let man and beast be covered with sackcloth and cry mightily unto God. Let them turn everyone from his evil way and from the violence that is in their hands." (Jonah 3:3-10)

This is where we are today. Later in the book we will show what the scripture says about sin and what happens when sin is finished. Proverbs 14:34 says, "Righteousness exalts a nation; sin is a reproach to any people." We want to emphasize this point, "Righteousness exalts a nation."

This is the missing link that many don't understand about this great nation of ours. America was built upon the principles of righteousness. This is what caused America to be exalted as a great nation. It was not solely because of the founders and forefathers and those that came afterward. Yes, they were a part of it because they believed in the principles and foundation of the

Almighty God and the Holy Scriptures. They believed in a power greater than themselves. It is not Capitalism that exalts a nation, it is righteousness.

Righteousness is, being in right standing with God. It does not mean right acting, but right standing. Only God can determine who is in right standing with Him. The scripture tells us that, "the eyes of the Lord are over the righteous, and His ears are opened to their cries" (1 Peter 3:12). There has been (and still are) many Nations with more capital than the United States, but they were not exalted as a great Nation or considered a super power.

Israel was named as God's chosen Nation, no one can argue with that. God declared it; therefore nothing can be done about it. However, there are many that disagree and desire to destroy Israel, not because of what Israel has or has not done but, primarily for this very reason; they are God's chosen people.

The message to the people of the world today is, we must change our culture in order to change our world. James 4:13 say, "Therefore to him that knoweth to do good, and doeth it not, to him it is sin". James 1:17 says, "Every good gift and every perfect gift is from above."

It is not about who is elected into office that will determine our destiny, it is us. It is each individual making a decision to do what is right in the sight of God. There is no law against love. As a matter of fact, real love cannot be legislated. Love covers a multitude of sin and so much more. Love will prevail. Love for God, Country and our fellowman.

Once on a radio program, the famed Dale Carnegie was asked to tell in three sentences the most important lesson he'd ever learned. He said, "The biggest lesson I have ever learned is the stupendous importance of what we think. If I knew what you think, I would know what you are, for your thoughts make you what you are. By changing our thoughts, we can change our lives."

If our thoughts can change our lives, I want to submit to you a word from the Lord: "By changing our culture, we can change our world.

INTRODUCTION

Oh taste and see that the Lord is good: blessed is the man that trustethin Him. Psalm 34:8 KJV

One of the first steps in changing your culture and your world is to repent and believe the gospel, (Mark 1:15.) The Bible says in Matthew 4:4 "Man shall not live by bread alone, but by every word that proceeds out of the mouth of God." The gospel is the truth of God's word or the good news concerning God's word. Many times, we have reservations or doubts about what God said He would do. Many of us believe that we don't believe as we should. In fact, we may not believe and trust God as we say we do.

In Mark 9:24 Jesus said to the man with the child that had a dumb spirit, "If thou canst believe, all things are possible to him that believe." The man said, "Lord I believe, but help my unbelief." He realized that he may have some doubt in his heart, to prevent him from receiving his miracle, he asked Jesus to help him with his unbelief.

The reality is; we do not know our own hearts as we think we do. If we look at Genesis 6:5, we see that our hearts can deceive us at any time if we are not careful.

This is the reason why the Bible tells us to guard and hide the word of God in our hearts that we might not sin against Him. To hide the word in our hearts is to read it, hear it, receive it, meditate upon it and let it not depart from us. We have to make it a part of the very essence of who we are.

Mark 4:15 says, immediately after the word is sown, Satan comes and tries to steal the word, so that it does not take root in you. Have you ever planted seeds in a garden or field and noticed soon after you planted the seeds the birds came and tried to pluck them out of the ground? The adversary knows if the word takes root in your heart it can grow and spring up to be a mighty tree (trees of righteousness). Therefore, his goal is to prevent the seed (word) from taking root in your heart.

The word "heart" here is not referring to our physical hearts; it is referring to the inner man (your spirit). The scripture speaks about being strengthened in your inner man (Ephesians 3:16) and "Out of your belly shall flow rivers of living waters" (John 7:38). These things speak about your spirit or man's spirit. It has always been the will of God for our inner man (spirit man), to rule and reign supreme over our soulish man (mind, will and emotions), because this is what the Holy Spirit connects to, Spirit to spirit.

Let us look at Thomas in John 20:25. Thomas is a person who walked with Christ as a disciple and an apostle. He was told by the other disciples (because he was not there when they saw Jesus) "We have seen the Lord" (John 20:19-24), But Thomas said to them, "Except I shall see in His hands the print of the nails, and put my finger into the print of the nails, and thrust my hand into His side, I will not believe." (John 20:25). Can you imagine this? Eight days later, the disciples were gathered together, this time Thomas was with them when Jesus appeared in the room (while the door was closed) and said "Peace be with you" (John 20:26).

Jesus began to speak to Thomas, He said, "Reach hither thy finger, and behold my hands; and reach hither thy hand, and thrust it into My side: and be not faithless but believing" (John 20:27). Jesus went on to say to Thomas, “because you have seen me, you believed, blessed are they that have not seen, and yet have believed." (John 20:29). Amazing, isn't it? For further study on the subjects: "Inner Man and Heart", I recommend these books, "The Spiritual Man" by Watchman Nee and "Matters of the Heart" by Prophetess Juanita Byuman. There may be other books out there but these are two I've read some years ago and was blessed by them on these subjects.

Chapter One

CULTURE DEFINED

Merriam-Webster Dictionary defines culture as: 1. the act of developing the intellectual and moral faculties especially by education. 2. The integrated pattern of human knowledge, belief, and behavior that depends upon the capacity for learning and transmitting knowledge to succeeding generations. 3. The customary beliefs, social forms, and material traits of a racial, religious, or social group; also: the characteristic features of everyday existence (as diversions or a way of life) shared by people in a place or time. In the book, “Fasting Made Easy” by Dr. Don Colbert M. D. he defines culture as a mindset of what one believes.

Culture affects our lives and the way we do things in life. In some Countries the strict adherence to cultural beliefs are of utmost importance, in many cases, breaking the practice of culture habits and traditions are extremely hard.

To some, their culture is the creed they live by because this is what they have been accustomed to all of their lives. It is a value they desire to pass on to their children and grandchildren. Culture is a lot like traditions in many regards; they both have their advantages and disadvantages and are sometimes misunderstood. We will talk more about both of these topics later in the book as we discover why it is important to; CHANGE YOUR CULTURE IN ORDER TO CHANGE YOUR WORLD

TRADITIONS

In this Country (USA) we deal more with traditions than with culture. Yes, there are some strong cultures here but for the most part as a whole we deal with traditions. The essences of traditions are; precepts passed down from past generations. If you look in the dictionary or do a quick search on the internet it will help you grasp what we mean concerning traditions. As a matter of fact, Wikipedia, the internet encyclopedia states, "tradition refers to beliefs, objects or customs performed or believed in the past, originating in it, transmitted through time by being taught by one generation to the next, and are performed or believed in the present." This is very similar to culture.

The problem with both culture and tradition is: they both have their origin and belief in something of the past which may not be based on truth. This can and may be causing problems for people in the present and the future. Sometimes because of culture and traditions, we may commit sins and offenses to God and not know it. This was a problem that the nation of Israel encountered.

Because we are not aware of these offenses, we never repent of them. This causes the same old cycles to continue, resulting in what we know as Generational Curses. In order to be delivered and set free from these curses, both the cycle and the curse must be broken and repentance must take place. Repentance means to have a change of mind, heart and direction, to turn away from one direction and go in a new or different direction.

SIN

Traditionally, most of us view sin as a two sided coin, on one side, sin is seen as an act or something we commit or do. The other side is blank, clear or clean which indicates, if we do not commit any of the acts, then there is no sin imputed. Unfortunately, that's not how it goes as far as the Kingdom of God is concerned. Although sin is sin no matter how you look at it, there are categories which sin falls into. The first category is: sins of Commission. The second is sins of Omission and the third is preconceived sins. The sin of Commission is as stated above. Committing an act or doing something we know we should not do but we choose to do it any way.

The scripture states in Colossians 3:25 (KJV) "But he that doeth wrong shall receive for the wrong which he hath done: and there is no respect of persons." We may often repent and ask for forgiveness of these sins when we realized we've sinned. Sins of Omissions are sins committed by not doing what we should have done. These often go un-repented of because they are not as obvious as the sins of Commission, so they create enormous mountains in our lives. James 4:17 gives a good example of this. "Therefore to him that knoweth to do good and doeth it not, to him it is sin."

THIRD CATEGORY

This third category called "Preconceived Sins," is not traditionally or theologically taught as a category of sin. When we read Matthew 5: 28, Jesus makes a statement that changes the dynamics of this subject, which is, sin and how it is committed.

Matthew 5:28 says, "But I say unto you, that whosoever looketh on a woman to lust after her hath committed adultery with her already in his heart." To get a complete picture of this statement we have to look at it starting with verse 27. In Matthew 5:27-28 (KJV) it says, "Ye have heard that it was said by them of old time, Thou shalt not commit adultery. But I say unto you, that whosoever looketh on a woman to lust after her hath committed adultery with her already in his heart."

This statement by Jesus in verse 27 goes to the core of what this book is about: Change your Culture, Change your World. In this verse Jesus makes reference to the fact that it was said by them of old time… (Representing culture, tradition) But

I say unto you…. (Whenever you make a statement and use the word "but" then continue on to make another statement, the word "but" cancels out the first statement, making the last statement first priority).

We want to be very clear; we are not in any way saying that the act of committing adultery is no longer a sin. Jesus said in Matthew 5:17, "Think not that I am come to destroy the law, or the prophets: I am not come to destroy, but to fulfill." When Jesus came on the scene, He raised the bar (the standard) creating a new category which includes lust, which is not an outward act as in the sins of Commission and Omission. James 1:15 says, "when lust hath conceived, it bringeth forth sin: and sin, when it is finished, bringeth forth death."

CHAPTER TWO

SEEK YE

But seek ye first the kingdom of God, and its righteousness, and all these things shall be added unto you. Matthew 6:33

Another step in changing your culture and your world is to apply the principles laid out in Matthew 6:33. This is a phenomenal passage of scripture with an awesome promise. All the promises of God are awesome and they are yea and amen, which means the answer of these promises is yes (you can have them) and amen which means "so be it or let it be done."

I believe many people have two main misconceptions as to the actual manifestations of this scripture (Matthew 6:33). (1) The misunderstanding of what it really means to "seek the kingdom of God and its righteousness." (2) The misunderstanding of the promises of God, which we will discuss later. Some would have you believe, to seek the kingdom of God only means to pray and ask God about your plans. To get a better understanding of this, let us look at the following words:

Seek: To go in search or quest of: to seek the truth, to search and attain the kingdom of God.

Search: To look at or examine (a person, object, etc.) carefully in order to find something concealed:

Government: The form or system of rule by which a state, community, etc., is governed:

Govern: To rule over by right of authority.

Kingdom of God: The spiritual domain over which God is sovereign, the government and rule of God.

Isaiah 9:6 says "and the government shall be upon his shoulder." This means that the responsibility to govern the whole earth will be upon Jesus' shoulder. When we think of shoulder in this term, we think of responsibilities, weights, or burdens being carried on the shoulders. In the Old Testament, the priests that carried the Ark of the Covenant, which represents the presence of God, were Sanctified men, holy and set apart. They carried the Ark of the Covenant on their shoulders (sanctified shoulders).

God solidified this through Jesus in Matthew 28:18 "All power is given unto me in heaven and in earth." (Also, see Daniel 7:13-14). All, means all with no exceptions. All powers that exist are ordained of God. "Let every soul be subject unto the higher powers. For there is no power but of God: the powers that be are ordained of God." (Romans 13:1).

The scriptures say God will make all mysteries known unto you. Who is He talking about? He is talking about His disciples, those who follow Him. Jesus makes it clear in Matthew 13:10-11 and Luke 8:10 that it is given unto the disciples to know the mysteries of both "The Kingdom of God" and "The Kingdom of Heaven."

When we sellout to God and act according to Matthew 6:33, He will reveal to us not only His will for our lives but also His will for the whole earth. Please keep in mind that with God, everything is on a need to know basis. If He determines that you don't need to know a certain thing at a certain point in time, He will not reveal it to you.

One of the reasons for this is found in John 16:12 that say, "I have yet many things to say to you, but you cannot bear them now." Meaning, you are not ready or equipped to handle more than you already know. When the time comes and He deems you are ready, He will reveal more to you. I've learned that much of this is based on what and who God called you to be.

God will not reveal to the pastor or teacher what He reveals to the Apostle and Prophet because the office and calls are different. You may say "I am an Apostle/Prophet just like you are an Apostle or Prophet. This may be true but our assignments are not the same.

Remember, Romans 8:28, “And we know that **all things work together for** good to them that love God, to them who are the called according to *His* purpose.”

For many years I thought I had a good working understanding of this scripture (Matthew 6:33). But one day the Holy Spirit quickened me and I became aware of what is known as "The 49 commands of Christ" (see index) and it all came together like a puzzle for me.

To seek the kingdom of God is to seek, to know and to understand the rule of God and the government of God. His righteousness is to put on His attributes, to become like Him, to have the mind of Christ in you. “Let this mind be in you that was also in Christ Jesus.” (Philippians 2:5).

The Bible says "be not conformed to this world but be ye transformed by the renewing of your mind, that ye may prove what *is* that good, acceptable, and perfect, will of God.” (Romans 12:2).

What happens at salvation and the new birth is, our spirit is renewed, regenerated and realigned so that it can receive the things of God/the Holy Spirit. Our soulish man (mind, will, and emotions) remains the same.

These things are not renewed or reborn, they have to be transformed by the renewing of our minds (growing and maturing in the things of God). Salvation is the first principle or doorway of the kingdom of God; it is not the end, as some believe. It allows you to enter into the kingdom of God and become a disciple of Christ, and then you must grow and mature in the stature, wisdom, grace, and knowledge of God

Romans 1:17 tells us that the righteousness of God is revealed from faith to faith and that the just shall live by faith. 2 Corinthians 3:18 (KJV) makes mention of us moving from glory to glory. In fact, the Message Bible says it this way "All of us, nothing between us and God, our faces shining with the brightness of His face. And so we are transfigured much like the Messiah, our lives gradually becoming brighter and more beautiful as God enters our lives and we become like Him."

The beauty of all of this can be found in Isaiah 28:9-11 which says, "Whom shall He teach knowledge? And whom shall He make to understand doctrine? *Them that are* weaned from the milk *and* drawn from the breasts. For precept *must be* upon precept, precept upon precept; line upon line, line upon line; here a little, *and* there a little: For with stammering lips and another tongue will He speak to this people." It is all a part of the nurturing plan of God to bring us to maturity in Him.

Mark 8:37 says, “what shall a man give in exchange for his soul?” Matthew 16:26 says, “For what is a man profited, if he shall gain the whole world and lose his soul?” Obviously the answer is nothing. The kingdom of God works by exchange; exchanging old theologies, thoughts and ideas for fresh new revelations from God to you via the Holy Spirit. It is the job of the Holy Spirit to lead us into **ALL TRUTHS,** not some truths or half-truths, but all truths.

John 16:13 makes this point very clear when it says, "Howbeit when He, the Spirit of truth, is come, He will guide you into **all truth**: for He shall not speak of Himself; but whatsoever He shall hear, *that* shall He speak: and He will shew you things to come."

This thought is expressed again in Mark 2:22 where it says, "And no man putteth **new wine** into old bottles: else the **new wine** doth burst the bottles, and the wine is spilled, and the bottles will be marred: but **new wine** must be put into new bottles." (Also see Matthew 9:17 and Luke 5:37-38). The meaning of this is; you cannot put new revelation on top of old revelation. The old must be cleared out (poured out) and replaced with the new, making the new revelation the foundation, as it is mentioned in Ephesians 2:20 "And are built upon the foundation of the apostles and prophets, Jesus Christ Himself being the chief corner *stone."*

The entire second chapter of Ephesians gives a great summation of this point.

"And you hath he quickened, who were dead in trespasses and sins; Wherein in time past ye walked according to the course of this world, according to the prince of the power of the air, the spirit that now worketh in the children of disobedience:

Among whom also we all had our conversation in times past in the lusts of our flesh, fulfilling the desires of the flesh and of the mind; and were by nature the children of wrath, even as others. But God, who is rich in mercy, for his great love wherewith he loved us,

Even when we were dead in sins, hath quickened us together with Christ, (by grace ye are saved ;) And hath raised us up together, and made us sit together in heavenly places in Christ Jesus

That in the ages to come he might shew the exceeding riches of his grace in his kindness toward us through Christ Jesus. For by grace are ye saved through faith; and that not of yourselves: it is the gift of God: Not of works, lest any man should boast.

For we are his workmanship, created in Christ Jesus unto good works, which God hath before ordained that we should walk in them.

Wherefore remember, that ye being in time past Gentiles in the flesh, who are called

Uncircumcision by that which is called the Circumcision in the flesh made by hands;

That at that time ye were without Christ, being aliens from the commonwealth of Israel, and strangers from the covenants of promise, having no hope, and without God in the world:

But now in Christ Jesus ye who sometimes were far off are made nigh by the blood of Christ.
For he is our peace, who hath made both one, and hath broken down the middle wall of partition between us;

Having abolished in his flesh the enmity, even the law of commandments contained in ordinances; for to make in himself of twain one new man, so making peace;

And that he might reconcile both unto God in one body by the cross, having slain the enmity thereby:
And came and preached peace to you which were afar off, and to them that were nigh.

For through him we both have access by one Spirit unto the Father.
Now therefore ye are no more strangers and foreigners, but fellow citizens with the saints, and of the household of God;

And are built upon the foundation of the apostles and prophets, Jesus Christ himself being the chief corner stone;

In whom all the building fitly framed together groweth unto an holy temple in the Lord:
In whom ye also are builded together for an habitation of God through the Spirit". Ephesians 2:1-22

SECOND MISCONCEPTION

The other misunderstanding many have is with the promises of God. Most of us know and often say, "The promises of God are yea and amen." So we develop a mindset that says, because the promises of God are yea and amen, they are automatically ours. Unfortunately this is not true.

Even though the promises are yea and amen, they are not automatic. Just as the kingdom works by exchange, so do the promises of God. They are contingent upon the terms and conditions being met. The Lord told Abram in Genesis 12 that He would bless him, make of him a great nation and his name would be great, but, Abram had to fulfill the terms and conditions of the promise, to make it come to pass, which are laid out in verse one.

"Now the LORD had said unto Abram, Get thee out of thy country, and from thy kindred, and from thy father's house, unto a land that I will shew thee:

And I will make of thee a great nation, and I will bless thee, and make thy name great; and thou shalt be a blessing:

And I will bless them that bless thee, and curse him that curseth thee: and in thee shall all families of the earth be blessed." Genesis 12:1-3

Fortunately for Abram, he obeyed the Lord as we read in verse four. In order for Abram to receive the blessings, he had to leave his father's house and his family. In Joshua 1:5-6, the Lord said to Joshua, "As I was with Moses, so will I be with you. Be strong and of good courage." Again, we see the conditions are set for the Lord to be with Joshua just as He was with Moses.

Joshua could have chosen not to be very courageous and said, "I'm going to do it my way," this would have denied him the opportunity to have the Lord with him just as He was with Moses.

We sometimes sing the song "Father Abraham had many sons, and many sons had Father Abraham, I am one of them and so are you...." Well, just because Father Abraham had many sons does not mean that all of them are heirs of the promise. Ishmael was one of Abraham's sons, but he was not the heir of the promise, Isaac was. Galatians 3:29 says, "If we be in Christ, then we are Abraham's seed, and heirs according to the promise."

The apostle Paul clarifies the mystery of the doctrine of Abraham's seed in Galatians 3:16. Many believe that just because they are in the faith and attend church they are Abraham's seed. The apostle Paul says this is not true. He said in Galatians 3:16, "Now to Abraham and his seed were the promises made. He saith not, and to seeds, as of many; but as of one," "And to thy seed," which is Christ."

This is a very important statement. Christ is Abraham's seed, not us. We become heirs of the promises to Abraham if we are in Christ. The conditions are; if we are in Christ, then we are Abraham's seed. Not, if we are in the church, then we are Abraham's seed.

The sad truth is, many of us that are in church are not in Christ, therefore we are disqualified for the promises of Abraham. This is not judgmental, condemnation, criticism or my personal opinion, this is actual scripture. This brings us back to the very subject of this book "Change your Culture, Change your World."

CHAPTER THREE

THE DIFFERENCE

And from the days of John the Baptist until now the kingdom of heaven suffereth violence, and the violent take it by force. Matthew 11:12

"**Come unto me**, all ye that labour and are heavy laden and I will give you rest." Matthew 11:28

We are living in a time where everything is changing at a rapid pace. Nothing is the same anymore. One of the main reasons for this is found in 2 Corinthians 4:4 which says, "In whom the god of this world hath blinded the minds of them which believe not, lest the light of the glorious gospel of Christ, who is the image of God, should shine unto them."

The god of this world has blinded the minds of them that believe not. This is a powerful statement for several reasons:
1. We must first understand who the god of this world is. 2. Why is this god focused on blinding the minds (not the eyes) of them that do not

believe? 3. What is it that they do not believe that would cause this to happen?

It is time for us to take a long hard look at the truth and learn to distinguish fact from truth and learn to apply these truths to our lives.

It is a fact that the god of this world is trying to blind the minds of all that he can, but the truth is, it does not have to happen to you. You can escape and overcome every tactic this god attempts to employ to blind your mind. 1 Corinthians 10:13 says, "There hath no temptation taken you but such as is common to man: but God is faithful, who will not suffer you to be tempted above that ye are able; but will with the temptation also make a way to escape, that ye may be able to bear it."

The Bible says in Proverbs 14:12 "There is a way which seemeth right unto a man, but the ends thereof are the ways of death."

Proverbs 16:2 says, "All the ways of a man are clean in his own eyes; but the LORD weigheth the spirits."

The god of this world is cunning and crafty; he does things in a subtle way. He does not play fair at all and has no regard for anyone or anything that stands in his way. Because of this, we have to make a change in the way we see, do and view things concerning the spirit realm and the Kingdom of God.

Luke 21:31 says, "So likewise ye, when ye see these things come to pass, know ye that the kingdom of God is nigh at hand". Matthew 3:2 says, "Repent ye: for the kingdom of heaven is at hand". Mark 1:15 says, "The time is fulfilled, and the kingdom of God is at hand: repent ye, and believe the gospel." Acts 3:19 says, "Repent ye therefore, and be converted, that your sins may be blotted out, when the times of refreshing shall come from the presence of the Lord."

It is time to make a change. Change from the current way we do things, especially those things that are not leading us to a closer relationship with Christ. Romans10:7 say, "Who shall descend into the deep? (That is, to bring up Christ again from the dead.). 1 Corinthians 2:10 But God hath revealed them unto us by His Spirit: for the Spirit searcheth all things, yea, and the deep things of God."

THE HEART OF GOD

God is seeking change in His people, for them not to be conformed to this world, but be transformed by the renewing of their minds. The renewing of the mind is to have a new mindset. A change in the way one views things, to see things from a Kingdom of God perspective. It is to accept as truth the things God reveals to you by the Holy Spirit. John 16:13 says "Howbeit when He, the Spirit of truth, is come, He will guide you into all truth: for He shall not speak of Himself; but whatsoever He shall hear, that shall He speak: and He will shew you things to come."

I believe it is equally important to mention the scripture quoted in John 14:17, which says, "Even the Spirit of truth; whom the world cannot receive, because it seeth him not, neither knoweth him: but ye know him; for he dwelleth with you, and shall be in you. " This scripture testifies to the fact that, if you are not born again of the Spirit and the water you cannot comprehend the things God is saying, because they are spiritually discerned.

Not only does He not want us to be conformed to this world, but also not conformed to the doctrine of men or the tradition of men. He wants us to be translated into the kingdom of His dear Son (1 Colossians 1:13). We want to emphasize here that when we mention "The Kingdom or Kingdom Culture" we are talking about the Kingdom of God. Not any other kingdom such as the kingdom of darkness or the kingdoms of this world. From this point on, we will be focusing on Matthew 11:12, to emphasize the importance of this scripture and the role it plays in our lives.

CHAPTER FOUR
THE DEBATE

In chapter fifteen of the book of Matthew (KJV), we read about a debate in which the scribes and Pharisees of Jerusalem came to Jesus to ask why His disciples transgress the traditions of the elders.

"Then came to Jesus scribes and Pharisees, which were of Jerusalem, saying, why do thy disciples transgress the tradition of the elders? For they wash not their hand s when they eat bread.

But he answered and said unto them, Why do ye also transgress the commandment of God by your tradition?

For God commanded, saying, Honour thy father and mother: and, He that curseth father or mother, let him die the death.

But ye say, whosoever shall say to his father or his mother, It is a gift, by whatsoever thou mightest be profited by me;

And honour not his father or his mother, he shall be free. Thus have ye made the commandment of God of none effect by your tradition"
Matthew 5:1-6

The scribes and Pharisees came to Jesus looking for an answer concerning tradition. The answer Jesus gave them was not what they expected. It hurt them to their hearts to learn their tradition made the word of God ineffective to them and those they taught. Let us hear the conclusion as Jesus is speaking to the scribes and Pharisees:

"Ye hypocrites, well did Esaias prophesy of you, saying,

This people draweth nigh unto me with their mouth, and honoureth me with their lips; but their heart is far from me.

But in vain they do worship me, teaching for doctrines the commandments of men.

And he called the multitude, and said unto them, Hear, and understand:

Not that which goeth into the mouth defileth a man; but that which cometh out of the mouth, this defileth a man.

Then came his disciples, and said unto him, Knowest thou that the Pharisees were offended, after they heard this saying?

But he answered and said, every plant, which my heavenly Father hath not planted, shall be rooted up.

Let them alone: they be blind leaders of the blind. And if the blind lead the blind, both shall fall into the ditch.

Then answered Peter and said unto him, Declare unto us this parable.

And Jesus said, Are ye also yet without understanding?

Do not ye yet understand, that whatsoever entereth in at the mouth goeth into the belly, and is cast out into the draught?

But those things which proceed out of the mouth come forth from the heart; and they defile the man.

"For out of the heart proceed evil thoughts, murders, adulteries, fornications, thefts, false witness, and blasphemies."

"These are the things which defile a man: but to eat with unwashen hands defileth not a man."
Matthew 15:7-20

What an amazing conclusion to this debate! Not only did Jesus answer their question concerning tradition, but He also addressed to the multitude of people the issue we previously stated. The issue we called preconceived sin or "matters of the heart."

Jesus did not stop there, He went on to clarify some things that were heavy on Peter's heart and mind. Peter asked Jesus in verse fifteen to explain to them what He meant by these sayings. Jesus responded to Peter sternly. He said, "Are you also yet without understanding?" Meaning, all the time you've been with me and you are still without understanding? Understand this, it is not what goes in the mouth that defiles a man, it is what comes out of the mouth that defiles a man. A lot of what we hear and learn in many churches today as doctrine are commandments of men, not commandments of God.

Interesting note: Why did Jesus refer to the Pharisees as "blind leaders of the blind?" When you are blind you cannot see anything. The Pharisees could not see their need for a Savior, nor recognize Jesus as the Christ (the anointed one). They could not see that they were sinners needing the grace of the Savior, yet they wanted to lead others.

Notes of Understanding

Proverbs 4:7 says, "And with all thy getting, get an understanding." It is very important that we get an understanding of some key factors before going further. We are going to take a look at several groups of people in Scripture that will help us better understand them and their roles of participation.

Pharisees

The Pharisees were a Jewish sect that belonged to a Jewish political party. They were upholders of tradition and sticklers for the Mosaic Law. They were very careful in outward details and appearance. They were rigid in fasting, zealous for Judaism, lovers of display, cruel persecutors, covetous and blind to spiritual things. They often opposed Jesus as He went about doing good.

Sadducees

The Sadducees were a Jewish religious sect of people in the time of Christ that believed only in the law and not oral tradition, like the Pharisees. They were in denial of the resurrection, immortality of the soul and spirit world. The Sadducees were supporters of the Maccabeans, which is a relatively small group, but they generally held the high priesthood. They were denounced by Jesus (Matthew 16:6-12), by John the Baptist (Matthew 3:7-12) and the apostolic church (Acts 5:17).

Samaritans

The Samaritans were inhabitants of Samaria made up of mixed races. They sought alliance with the Jews and offered to help in the rebuilding of the wall, but were rejected by Nehemiah. They believed that the Messiah which is called Christ would one day come and He would tell them all things. Many of the Samaritans were converted through the preaching of the gospel by Phillip the evangelist.

Scribes

The Scribes were experts in legal matters. They were transcribers of legal contracts, keepers of records, advisers in state affairs, teachers of the law and collectors of temple revenue. Like the Pharisees, their righteousness was external and they taught without authority. Their attitudes towards Christ were of accusation and questioning of His authority. They even accused Christ of blasphemy. Christ's attitude towards them was that they were hypocrites that needed to be exposed and condemned.

CHAPTER FIVE

The Woman at the Well

This is from a very familiar passage of scripture found in the gospel of St. John chapter four, where Jesus enters a conversation with a woman of Samaria. There are many interesting points about this passage and its message to which many people still have questions about to this day.

Many sermons have been preached, arguments made and books and articles written trying to understand the real significance of why Jesus said that it was necessary for Him to go through Samaria from Judea to get to His base in Galilee. Some of the Catholics say the reason for the journey this way was to avoid the Pharisees who often opposed Him and His mission. Well, the truth is, Jesus being the son of God and knowing all things, even the thoughts and intents of the heart, knew that it was time to bring to an end a long-standing tradition and culture among the Jews and Samaritan people.

The Story

When the Lord Jesus found out that the Pharisees had heard that He (Jesus) made and baptized more disciples than John (although Jesus did not baptize any of them Himself, His disciples did) He knew it was time to leave Judaea and head back to Galilee. Jesus felt the need to pass through Samaria (some scholars say that it was not necessary for Jesus to go through Samaria, He could have gone another way).

When Jesus arrived in a city of Samaria called Sychar (Sichar, the Capital of Samaria) He was thirsty and wearied from the journey. He came to a well, known as Jacob's well and began to sit down to rest on the well. It was about the sixth hour (noontime) when a Samaritan woman came to the well to draw water. Jesus said to the woman, "Give me to drink."

She replied to Him "How is it that thou, being a Jew, askest drink of me, which is a woman of Samaria?" For the Jews have no dealings with the Samaritans. Jesus replied to the woman and said

"If thou knewest the gift of God, and who it is that saith to thee, Give me to drink; thou would have asked of Him, and He would have given thee living water."

Let's pause here a moment and bring some things into focus. I'm sure when the woman arrived at the well she recognized the man sitting on the well was a Jew. She knew the Jews and the Samaritans had no dealings, yet she did not feel threatened or the need to be alarmed just because a Jewish man was sitting on the well.

Verse ten of this chapter gives us a sneak peek into the purpose of Jesus journey to Samaria when He said, "If thou knew the gift of God, and who it is that saith to thee…"

One would have to ask a couple of questions here to obtain clarity of the message. The first question would be; what is the gift of God? And the second one would be; how is this gift given? The answers are; the gift of God is eternal life and it is given through Jesus Christ our Lord. Jesus was saying to the woman: "I came to give you life and give it to you more abundantly."

Obviously, the woman did not have spiritual ears to hear what the Spirit was saying to her, because she proceeded to say to Jesus that He had nothing to draw the water with and that the well was deep. However, she heard enough to want to know where this living water was coming from. As the conversation continued, the woman was convinced that she needed this water. She said to Jesus, “Sir, give me this water, that I thirst not and neither come hither to draw.”

The Culture Change

This conversation was only the first part of Jesus’s mission to Jacob’s well in Samaria. After the request of the woman for this living water which Jesus would gladly oblige, He said to her, go call your husband and tell him to come here. The woman said to Jesus, “I have no husband.” Jesus said to her, “You have well said, you have no husband.” Meaning, you are telling the truth, but, you had five husbands in the past and the one you are with now is not your husband. Wow! What a way to bring the truth.

This is very intriguing. Why would Jesus, being all knowing, ask her this question when He already knew the answer? The answer is simple. 1. To reveal to her that He knew things about her that only she knew. 2. To confirm to her what she already believed concerning the Messiah. The woman informed Jesus that she knew that one day the Messiah which is called Christ would come and He would tell them all things. Jesus said to her "I that speakest to thee am He."

What is even more interesting is when the disciples returned from buying bread in the city, they came upon Jesus talking to the Samaritan woman. They were all amazed, yet not one of them said anything. They just marveled to themselves. No one said to the woman, "what seeketh thou?" Or to Jesus, "why thou talketh to her?" At that point, the woman left her water pot, and went her way into the city and said to the men: come see a man, which told me all things I ever did. Is not this the Christ?

The disciples knew the culture was that the Samaritans had no dealings with the Jews. They also knew Jesus never did anything without a cause. So when they saw Jesus talking to the Samaritan woman, they knew there had to be a reason behind it. They may not have known the reason then, but they knew there was one.

To understand why the Jews and the Samaritans despised one another, you would have to go back as far as 721 BC, when the Assyrians invaded the Northern Kingdom and scattered them among other groups that were already scattered. This action caused a division in the Northern Kingdom. The Samaritans believed they were the true believers and heirs of Abraham, Isaac and Jacob. To the Jews, the Samaritans were responsible for the two worst abominations ever: Schism (division) and Idolatry. In Luke 9:15 Jesus called James and his brother John, Boanerges (which means, sons of thunder) because they wanted to call down fire from heaven to destroy some Samaritans in a certain village. The issues and unrest between the Jews and the Samaritans continued from that time (721 BC) to the day Jesus met the woman at the well. What was so significant about that day, that woman and the well?

CHAPTER SIX

The Mystery Revealed

What the Lord revealed to us through the Holy Spirit: the reason Jesus said that He needed to go through Samaria was; in order to change a world (two worlds, Jews and Samaritans) there had to be a change in culture. The Jews and Samaritans had no dealings with one another for generations. Jesus broke this tradition and brought a change to the culture by initiating a conversation with the Samaritan woman. By engaging in the conversation with Jesus, she was able to secure eternal life (1 Timothy 6:12). She received both, the living water Jesus told her about and the abundant life.

Not only did the woman receive salvation (living water) and abundant life but, she was also one of the first people given the great commission to go make disciples. This led to a change in tradition and culture in other areas, the areas of women keeping silent and not preaching or spreading the gospel.

Let us continue to look at this amazing story as it reveals more great truths starting at John 4:29 where the woman went into the city saying, " Come, see a man, which told me all things that ever I did: is not this the Christ?" This was a great commission cry to make disciples, to give others the opportunity to receive this same living water and to partake in abundant life.

John 4:30 says, "Then they went out of the city, and came unto Him. In the mean while His disciples prayed him, saying, "Master, eat. But He said unto them, "I have meat to eat that ye know not of." Therefore said the disciples one to another, Hath any man brought Him ought to eat? Jesus saith unto them, My meat is to do the will of Him that sent me and to finish His work." In other words, this is the reason we are here at this well.

In John 4:35, Jesus said to the disciples: "Say not ye, There are yet four months, and then cometh harvest? Behold, I say unto you, Lift up your eyes, and look on the fields; for they are white already to harvest." This is a very powerful point. When Jesus and the disciples were having this conversation, the woman had not yet returned from the city with the people. The disciples could not see in the Spirit what Jesus meant when He told them to lift up their eyes and look on the fields for they are white already to harvest.
What He was saying to them was, any minute now this scripture will be fulfilled this day.

Jesus makes an interesting analysis in John 4:36 He tells the disciples, "He that reapeth receiveth wages, and gathereth fruit unto life eternal: that both he that soweth and he that reapeth may rejoice together." Wow! What an amazing principle! The disciples reaped the wages of a harvest from Jesus sowing the word into the woman, because they were with Jesus on this mission.

The people that came from the city received wages of eternal life because they received the word (Jesus). The woman received wages of souls won into the Kingdom of God because of her sowing the message ("come see a man") into the lives of the people in the city. John 4:37 says, "And herein is that saying true, One soweth, and another reapeth." Now they all rejoiced together the sowers and the reapers, making this a win/win for everyone involved.

In John 4:39 it says, "and many of the Samaritans of that city believed on Him for the saying of the woman, which testified, He told me all that ever I did." John 4:40, says "So when the Samaritans were come unto Him, they besought Him that He would tarry with them: and He abode there two days." John 4:41 says, "and many more believed because of His own word; and said unto the woman, Now we believe, not because of thy saying: for we have heard Him ourselves, and know that this is indeed the Christ, the Savior of the world."

Here we see the issue of "male verses female," similar to some of the traditions and culture we have in many areas in this day and time. John 4:39 says, "Many of the Samaritans of that city believed on Him because of the sayings of the woman." I believe that this group may have been made up of the women and few men. You see, most women do not have an issue with other women preaching, pastoring or exercising their gift or calling in the Lord.

It is a small group in the community of believers that have an issue with this mainly because of culture and traditions that have been handed down from generation to generation. This is a Pharisee spirit. Jesus told the Pharisees that their traditions made the word of God have no effect.

It is evident that the men of Samaria had a problem with this. We read in John 4:41 where it says, "and many more believed because of his own word; and said unto the woman, Now we believe, not because of thy saying: for we have heard Him ourselves, and know that this is indeed the Christ, the Saviour of the world."

I believe that this "many more" may have been men with their egos and pride, not wanting to receive this message because it was delivered by a woman. What a terrible thing to say to the woman, "now we believe, not because you said, but, because we heard it ourselves."

Okay, wonderful. I'm glad you heard and received, but the truth is, had the woman not gone into the city crying "come see a man who told me all things I ever did;" there would not have been a reason for them to go out and see for themselves.

The Bible says in John 4:24, "God is a Spirit: and they that worship Him must worship Him in spirit and in truth." The words of Jesus are Spirit and it gives life to all that receive it. It is time that we change our culture and tradition in this regard. Galatians 3:28 says, "There is neither Jew nor Greek, there is neither bond nor free, there is neither male nor female: for ye are all one in Christ Jesus."

Jesus said in Matthew 10:40, "He that receiveth you receiveth me, and he that receiveth me receiveth Him that sent me." Luke 10:16, "He that heareth you heareth me; and he that despiseth you despiseth me; and he that despiseth me despiseth Him that sent me." Isaiah 11:6, "and a little child shall lead them." Mark 9:37, "whosoever shall receive one of such children in my name, receiveth me: and whosoever shall receive me, receiveth not me, but him that sent me."

Luke 9:48, "And said unto them, whosoever shall receive this child in my name receiveth me: and whosoever shall receive me receiveth him that sent me: for he that is least among you all, the same shall be great." John 5:24, "Verily, verily, I say unto you, He that heareth my word, and believeth on him that sent me, hath everlasting life, and shall not come into condemnation; but is passed from death unto life."

All of these points speak to the fact that God is seeking a people that have ears to hear what the Spirit says to the church (the temple, your temple). The scripture says that "the time will come, and now is when the true worshippers must worship Him in Spirit and in truth: for the Father seeks such to worship Him" (John 4:23).

Jesus said, "my sheep hear my voice, and I know them, and they follow me" (John 10:27).

What this scripture says is, it does not matter whether it is male or female that is speaking the words. What matters is; is it a vessel that is authorized (ordained, anointed and called of God) to speak, carry or deliver the message given to them? God is a Spirit. We are speaking spirits. We are to carry out the divine assignments given us by God through Jesus Christ and the Holy Spirit. To be obedient to the call of God on our lives just as Jesus was obedient even to the death of the cross.

John 15:16 says, "Ye have not chosen me, but I have chosen you, and ordained you, that ye should go and bring forth fruit, and that your fruit should remain: that whatsoever ye shall ask of the Father in my name, he may give it you."

I often say to people when asked my position on this matter; "if you are lost in the woods and are trying to find your way home, would it matter to you who finds you (male or female) and points you in the right direction?" The answer to that question is no. It really would not matter, just as long as you get home or where you need to be. This is the same position Jesus took with this issue. All that matters at the end of the day is what Jesus said.

Psalms 107:20 says, "He sent his word, and healed them, and delivered them from their destructions." This passage of scripture does not say who or how He sent His word. What it implies is, His word was sent to accomplish a mission (to heal and deliver from destruction) and the people received the word and were healed.

There are many arguments made concerning this matter. Some say that "a woman is not supposed to preach." Some say, "A woman is not supposed to usurp the authority of a man." Others say, "When a woman steps behind the sacred desk (pulpit), she usurps the authority over the man." All of these sayings in this context are ridiculous and have no place in Christ.

You may say, some of this is truth or part truth anyway. But, you must remember that half-truth or part truth is a whole lie. True, God did not call a woman to usurp the authority over a man; neither did He call a man to usurp the authority over another man for that matter. When Jesus (as a man) walked the earth, He did not force or make His disciples follow Him against their will.

He said to them in Matthew 4:19, "Follow me, and I will make you fishers of men." He put it another way in Mark 1:17, "And Jesus said unto them, Come ye after me, and I will make you to become fishers of men." In other words, He will teach them how to become fishers of men. They were already skilled in the craft of fishing to support their families. Jesus wanted to disciple them in fishing for men. They had a choice in the matter. They could have refused the offer and allowed it to pass on to someone else, but because they had ears to hear they took Him up on the opportunity.

Here is something that is very interesting. In Matthew 28 it talks about the resurrection of Christ and the things that took place on that day. Verse one says, "In the end of the Sabbath, as it began to dawn toward the first day of the week, came Mary Magdalene and the other Mary to see the sepulchre."

Matthew 28:2 says, "and, behold, there was a great earthquake: for the angel of the Lord descended from heaven, and came and rolled back the stone from the door, and sat upon it." Matthew 28:3 says, "His countenance was like lightning, and his raiment white as snow."

Matthew 28:4 says, "And for fear of him the keepers did shake, and became as dead men". Matthew 28:5 says, "And the angel answered and said unto the women, Fear not ye: for I know that ye seek Jesus, which was crucified".

Matthew 28:6 says, "He is not here: for He is risen, as He said. Come; see the place where the Lord lay". Matthew 28:7 says, "and go quickly, and tell his disciples that He is risen from the dead; and, behold, He goeth before you into Galilee; there shall ye see Him: lo, I have told you". Matthew

28:8 says, "And they departed quickly from the sepulchre with fear and great joy; and did run to bring His disciples word".

So much can be said about this passage. The angel of the Lord gave the message to the women to deliver to the men (disciples) what to do. You may have noticed in verse four that the keepers of the tomb (men) became fearful and began to shake and became as dead men.

Matthew 28:9, "And as they went to tell his disciples, behold, Jesus met them, saying, All hail. And they came and held Him by the feet, and worshipped Him." Matthew 28:10 says, "Then said Jesus unto them, Be not afraid: go tell my brethren that they go into Galilee, and there shall they see me."

Here, we see that not only did the angel commission them to go and deliver the message, but, Jesus Himself gave instructions to the women, commissioning them to go and deliver the message; to carry out the assignment He had given them. Verse nine says, that they came and held Him by the feet and worshipped Him, indicating that they were not afraid.

Verse ten states that Jesus said to them, "be not afraid." He did not tell them this because they were afraid of Him, but to assure them they had His authority to carry out this assignment.

As we read further in the story we will see the reaction of the disciples when they encounter Jesus. Matthew 28:16, "Then the eleven disciples went away into Galilee, into a mountain where Jesus had appointed them. And when they saw Him, they worshipped Him: but some doubted." These are men that walked with Jesus and spent much of their time with Him, yet some of them doubted that it was Jesus.

CHAPTER SEVEN

LIFE AFTER THE ENCOUNTER

From Sinner to Saint

Who was the Samaritan woman at the well? The original name of the Samaritan woman is not known, but the church knows her as Photina (Svetlana in Russian). She was baptized after the resurrection, and, in a continuation of her zealous apostolic ministry that begun on the day she met the Lord, She preached in many areas, including Carthage and Smyrna in Asia Minor, where she was martyred. She is commemorated February 28th, and, of course, on the fifth Sunday of Pascha.

"The holy martyr Photina (Svetlana) was that Samaritan woman who had the rare fortune to speak with the Lord Christ Himself at Jacob's Well in Sychar (John. 4). Coming to faith in the Lord, she then came to believe in His Gospel, together with her two sons, Victor and Josiah, and five sisters who were called Anatolia, Phota, Photida, Paraskeva and Kyriake .

They went to Carthage in Africa, but they were arrested and taken to Rome in the time of the Emperor Nero, and thrown into prison. By the providence of God, Domnina, Nero's daughter, came into contact with St. Photina and was brought by her to the Christian faith. After imprisonment, they all suffered for Christ. Photina, who first encountered the light of truth by a well, was thrown into a well, where she died and entered into the immortal Kingdom of Christ.

Holy Martyr Photina of Samaria

The New Testament describes the familiar account of the "woman at the well" (John 4:5-42), who was a Samaritan. Up to that point she had led a sinful life, one which resulted in a rebuke from Jesus Christ. However, she responded to Christ's stern admonition with genuine repentance, was forgiven her sinful ways, and became a convert to the Christian Faith - taking the name 'Photina' at Baptism, which literally means "the enlightened one."

A significant figure in the Johannine community, the Samaritan Woman, like many other women, contributed to the spread of Christianity. She therefore occupies a place of honor among the apostles. In Greek sermons from the fourth to the fourteenth centuries she is called "apostle" and "evangelist." In these sermons, the Samaritan Woman is often compared to the male disciples and apostles and found to surpass them.

Later, Byzantine hagiographers developed the story of the Samaritan Woman, beginning where Saint John left off. At Pentecost Saint, Photina received baptism, along with her five sisters, Anatole, Photo, Photis, Paraskeve, Kyriake, and her two sons, Photeinos and Joseph. She then began a missionary career, traveling far and wide, preaching the good news of the Messiah's coming, His death and resurrection. When Nero, the emperor of Rome, began to persecute Christians, Photina and her son Joseph were in Carthage, in Africa, where she was preaching the Christian gospel.

After Jesus appeared to Photina in a dream, she sailed to Rome. Her son and many Christians from Africa accompanied her. Photina arrival and activity aroused curiosity in the capital city. Everyone talked about her.

"**Who is this woman?**" they asked. "She came here with a crowd of followers and she preaches Christ with great boldness." Soldiers were ordered to bring her to the emperor, but Photina anticipated them. Before they could arrest her, Photina, with her son Joseph and her Christian friends, went to Nero.

When the emperor saw them, he asked why they had come. Photina answered, "We have come to teach you to believe in Christ." The half-mad ruler of the Roman Empire did not frighten her. She wanted to convert him! Nero asked the saints their names. Again Photina answered.

By name she introduced herself, her five sisters and younger son. The emperor then demanded to know whether they had all agreed to die for the Nazarene. Photina spoke for them. “Yes, for the love of Him we rejoice and in His name we'll gladly die.” Hearing their defiant words, Nero ordered their hands beaten with iron rods for three hours.

At the end of each hour another persecutor took up the beating. The saints, however, felt no pain. Nothing happened to their hands. Photina joyfully quoted words of a psalm by David: “God is my help. No matter what anyone does to me, I shall not be afraid.” Perplexed by the Christian's endurance and confidence, Nero ordered the men thrown into jail.

Photina and her five sisters were brought to the golden reception hall in the imperial palace. There, the six women were seated on golden thrones, In front of them stood a large golden table covered with gold coins, jewels and dresses. Nero hoped to tempt the women by this display of wealth and luxury.

Nero then ordered his daughter Domnina, with her slave girls, to go speak with the Christian women. Women, he thought, would succeed in persuading their Christian sisters to deny their God.

Domnina greeted Photina graciously, mentioning the name of Christ. On hearing the princess' greeting, the saint thanked God. She then embraced and kissed Domnina. The women talked. But, the outcome of the women's talk was not what Nero wished.

Photina catechized Domnina and her hundred slave girls and baptized them all. She gave the name Anthousa to Nero's daughter. After her baptism, Anthousa immediately ordered all the gold and jewels on the golden table distributed to the poor of Rome. When the emperor heard that his own daughter had been converted to Christianity, he condemned Photina and all her companions to death by fire.

For seven days the furnace burned, but when the door of the furnace was opened, it was seen that the fire had not harmed the saints. Next the emperor tried to destroy the saints with poison, Photina offered to be the first to drink it. "O King," she said, "I will drink the poison first so that you might see the power of my Christ and God."

All the saints then drank the poison after her. None suffered any ill effects from it. In vain Nero subjected Photini, her sisters, sons and friends to every known torture. The saints survived unscathed to taunt and ridicule their persecutor.

For three years they were held in a Roman prison. Saint Photina transformed it into a "house of God." Many Romans came to the prison, were converted and baptized. Finally, the enraged tyrant had all the saints, except for Photini, beheaded. She was thrown first into a deep, dry well and then into prison again.

Photina now grieved that she was alone, that she had not received the crown of martyrdom together with her five sisters, Anatole, Photo, Photis, Paraskeve and Kyriake and her two sons, Photeinos and Joseph. Night and day she prayed for release from this life. One night, God appeared to her, made the sign of the cross over her three times.

For generation after generation, Orthodox Christians have addressed this prayer to the woman exalted by the Messiah when He sat by the well in Samaria and talked with her: TROPARION Hymn in tone 3: All illuminated by the Holy Spirit, you drank with great and ardent longing of the waters Christ the Savior gave to you; and with the streams of salvation you were refreshed, which you abundantly gave to those athirst. O Great Martyr and true peer of the Apostles, Photina, entreat Christ God to grant mercy to us.

KONTAKION Hymn in tone 3: Photina the glorious, the crown and glory of Martyrs, has this day ascended to the shining mansions of Heaven, and she called all together to sing her praises, that they might be recompensed with her hallowed graces. Let us all with faith and longing extol her gladly in hymns of triumph and joy! (Adapted from, Saints and sisterhood: The lives of forty-eight Holy Women Light and Life Publishing Company. (Used by permission)

CHAPTER EIGHT

THE MIND OF GOD

For who hath known the mind of the Lord? Or who hath been his counsellor? Romans 11:34. For who hath known the mind of the Lord, that he may instruct him? But we have the mind of Christ. 1 Corinthians 2:16.

I believe that we all would agree that the answer to the second part of both questions would be "no one." The Apostle Paul states in 1 Corinthians 2:16, "But we have the mind of Christ." This is a fascinating passage of scripture because it informs us that we (Those who have accepted the Lord Jesus Christ as savior) have the mind of Christ, which is able to make all things known to us through the Holy Spirit.

The mind of God is for us to become one in Christ. In John 17:11 &21, Jesus prayed to the Father, "Father, make them one as you and I are one." When we become one in Christ, there is no division among us. We would have the same goal, which is to please the Father.

The best and preferred way to please the Father is to love and heed the instructions of the Son (Jesus). In Matthew 22:37, a lawyer was trying to tempt Jesus with this question. "Which is the greatest commandment in the law?" Jesus said, "Thou shalt love the Lord thy God with all thy heart, and with all thy soul, and with all thy mind."

Jesus goes on to say, "This is the first and great commandment. And the second is like unto it, Thou shalt love thy neighbour as thyself." He continued saying, "On these two commandments hang all the law and the prophets." Matthew 22: 38-40.

Jesus could have gone on with a third and a fourth; but there was no need to do so, because all of the law and prophets could be summed up in these two commandments. There is no law against love. In fact the scripture says in 1 Peter 4:8 "Charity (love) covers a multitude of sin." Every time I would quote this scripture, the Holy Spirit would say to me "and so much more."

You see, only God knows how much love really covers and protects. There is a song that says, "When nothing else could help, love lifted me." If you listen to the testimonies' of people that have been delivered from cults, they all have one thing in common. They say that it was the love of the people that witnessed to them that caused them to give their lives to Christ.

There was a popular television soap opera years ago called, "Love is a Many Splendid Thing." When it came on, my mother and aunts would stop what they were doing and go watch it. I did not understand why this show had that kind of effect on them then.

Some years later, the Soulful singer Al Green came out with a hit song called "Love and Happiness". In his song he said, "Love will make you do wrong, love will make you do right, and love will make you stay out all night." Well, I surely did not understand that. What kind of unstable love would cause you to do such things? These are examples of how the world sees love but God has a different perspective on love and it challenges what the world tells us we should do.

I don't know what kind of love Al Green was talking about, but he clearly could not have been talking about the same kind of love Peter was talking about in 1 Peter 4:8.

The scripture says in Jeremiah 31:33, "But this shall be the covenant that I will make with the house of Israel; After those days, saith the LORD, I will put my law in their inward parts, and write it in their hearts; and will be their God, and they shall be my people."

THE JEWS AND THE GREEKS

"For there is no difference between the Jew and the Greek: for the same Lord over all is rich unto all that call upon him." Romans 10:12. When the Holy Spirit began to speak to me about this topic several months ago, He began to share with me that in the Kingdom of God there is no difference in the people.

I said, "Lord, I do not understand what you are saying." He took me to the scripture stated above and began to say, "Tell my people that there is no difference in one group verses another group that is in Christ."

The revelation of this is: for everyone that name's the name of the Lord is the same. We all belong to the Lord, and there is no one group that is superior to the other. He is the same Lord over all, and is able to deliver us all to our expected end. The culture of thinking that one group better than another group must end.

Just as the scripture says, there is no difference in the Jews and the Greeks; there is no difference in the Africans and the Asians, and there is no difference in the Americans and the Angolans that are in Christ. He is the same Lord over all. The same standard that applies to one applies to all.

No one should feel threatened, intimidated or unsafe in the company or presence of anyone who calls on the name of the Lord, regardless of who they are, where they are from, their race or nationality. If this exists in anyone that names the name of the Lord or claims to be in the Kingdom of God, the truth is not in them. They are of their father, the devil.

David said in Psalms 122:1, "I was glad when they said unto me, Let us go into the house of the LORD." David knew he could find peace and comfort as well as the answers he needed in the house of the Lord. No matter what tribes came up or went down, the house of the Lord should be the same as the name of the Lord. It should be a place where the righteous can run into it and are safe.

CHAPTER NINE

SPIRITUAL GIFTS

"Now concerning spiritual gifts, brethren, I would not have you ignorant. Ye know that ye were Gentiles, carried away unto these dumb idols, even as ye were led. Wherefore I give you to understand, that no man speaking by the Spirit of God calleth Jesus accursed: and that no man can say that Jesus is the Lord, but by the Holy Ghost." 1 Corinthians 12:1-3.

Concerning spiritual gifts, brethren, I would not have you ignorant. Why? The reason the apostle Paul said this can be found in Ephesians 2:11-15 which summarizes the fact that we were, at one time, far from Him but now we are made to be close to Him because of the blood of Jesus. He has also broken down the middle wall of partition between us. This is to say, we ourselves were lost at one time, but because of Him, we are found.

Now that we are made to be close to Him, we can partake in the spiritual gifts that are given to every man to profit thereby. 1 Corinthians 12:4-7 states:

"Now there are diversities of gifts, but the same Spirit. And there are differences of administrations, but the same Lord. And there are diversities of operations, but it is the same God which worketh all in all. But the manifestation of the Spirit is given to every man to profit withal."

In verse eight of the same chapter; it begins to list the different gifts. Verse ten mentions the "discerning of spirits." This is key to where we are today in the Spirit realm. This is very important, and I believe that the greatest of these gifts today is discernment. We have gotten away from using our discernment. The Bible says "follow charity and desire spiritual gifts." It says that for a reason. Many of us would rather spend our time seeking knowledge and information than seeking the gift of discernment.

An example of this I often use is that of the children of Issachar. In 1 Chronicles 12:32 it says, "And the children of Issachar were men that had understanding of the times, to know what Israel ought to do: the head of them were two hundred; and all their brethren were at their commandment." This is a magnificent passage of scripture.

Out of all the (population) people in Israel at the time, only about two hundred of them knew what Israel ought to do. They could discern the signs of the times and instruct the rest of the people what to do in order to line up with the will of the Lord.

In I Corinthians 14:1-2 the Apostle Paul says, "Follow (seek) after charity, and desire spiritual gifts, but rather that ye may prophesy (preach infallibly)." Here, the Apostle Paul expresses the superiority of the gift of prophecy, and gives this explanation in verse 3. "But he that prophesieth speaketh unto men to edification, (building up), exhortation and comfort."

I John 4:1 speak of the necessity of spiritual discernment (gift of discernment). It says, "Beloved, believe (trust) not every spirit, but try (prove, or test) the spirits whether they are of God; because many false prophets are gone out into the world." Here we see that discernment is a gift given by God for our protection and best interest.

Some of the greatest heroes in the Bible saw the need for this gift and sought for it. King Solomon requested this gift in I Kings 3. This is a powerful passage of scripture. Before we get to the passage of scripture let us set the stage leading up to this powerful passage.

I Kings 3:3

The Bible says in verse five, "While Solomon was in Gideon the Lord appeared to him in a dream by night and God said (to Solomon), ask what I shall give thee."

Wow! Solomon was in such a position of favor that the Lord God Himself appeared to him (in a dream) and asked him what he wanted to be given to him. This would be the time when most people would ask for the moon, stars, and everything else available.

Solomon did not do that. This is what he said, "Thou (you Lord) hast showed unto thy servant David my father great mercy, according as he walked before thee in truth, and in righteousness, and in uprightness of heart with thee; and thou hast kept for him this great kindness, that thou hast given him a son to sit on his throne, as *it is* this day. And now, O LORD my God, thou hast made thy servant king instead of David my father: and I *am* *but* a little child: I know not *how* to go out or come in. And thy servant *is* in the midst of thy people which thou hast chosen, a great people that cannot be numbered nor counted for multitude."

Verse 9 says, "Give therefore thy servant an understanding heart to judge thy people, that I may DISCERN between good and bad: for who is able to judge this thy so great a people." Amazing! The scripture says, "That the speech pleased the Lord, that Solomon asked this thing."

Look at the Lord's reply to his request. "And God said unto him, Because thou hast asked this thing, and hast not asked for thyself long life; neither hast asked riches for thyself, nor hast asked the life of thine enemies; but hast asked for thyself understanding to discern judgment; Behold, I have done according to thy words: lo, I have given thee a wise and an understanding heart; so that there was none like thee before thee, neither after thee shall any arise like unto thee." 1 Kings 3:9-12

The Lord granted Solomon his request for discernment and judgment. But, He did not stop there, He went on to say, **"And I have also given**

thee that which thou hast not asked, both riches, and honour: so that there shall not be any among the kings like unto thee all thy days." 1 Kings 3:13. The Lord gave Solomon more than what he requested.

This is the kind of thing we would hear older people talking about when we were growing up, a good measure (extra measure), or as they say in Louisiana, "Lagniappe." The Bible speaks of "Good measure, pressed down, shaken together and running over," surely, this is that.

God gave Solomon provisions to make up for his past, present and future. Then He laid it on even thicker for Solomon's long term future in verse 14. God said to Solomon "And if thou wilt walk in my ways, to keep my statutes and my commandments, as thy father David did walk, then I will lengthen thy days." 1 kings 3:14.

"For I know the plans I have for you, declares the LORD, "plans to prosper you and not to harm you, plans to give you hope and a future." (Jeremiah 29:11, NIV). Wow! The good future Solomon hoped for was extended by the grace of the Lord.

King David prayed for discernment in Psalm 119:18-19. His prayer was: "Open thou mine eyes, that I may behold wondrous things out of thy law. I am a stranger in the earth; hide not thy commandments from me."

Daniel sought for discernment in Daniel 7:15-16. "I Daniel was grieved in my spirit in the mist of my body, and the visions of my head troubled me.

I came near to one of them (angels) that stood by, and asked him the truth of all this. So he told me and made me know the interpretation of the things."

"FOR THIS CAUSE"

A few years ago the Lord revealed to us through the Holy Spirit a revelation concerning the passage of scripture in 1 Corinthians 11:30. He said "For this cause many *are* weak and sickly among you, and many sleep." He went on to explain the meaning of this revelation. He said these people did not seek out or discern who's who in the body of Christ. The Bible says, for the body has many members not of the same office to perform different functions.

God placed these gifts (the fivefold ministry) in the body (the church) for the perfection of the body. The Lord was saying to us, because many people had not distinguished who's who in the body of Christ, they are sickly and some sleep (dead).

To put it more plainly, there is no such thing as "one fold ministry" to perfect the body. Meaning the pastor alone cannot do it. Furthermore, none of the other remaining gifts (prophet, teacher, and evangelist) can activate the gift or call of God on your life, only the Apostle/Apostolic can. Yes, the Prophet can prophesy your future, gift or call on your life, but without the apostolic mantle, he/she cannot activate it.

The pastor, teacher, or evangelist may acknowledge that God has a call on your life, but that's the furthest they can go with it. Once the gift or call has been activated by the apostolic, the prophet can prophesy or foresee things concerning the future or give a word from the Lord concerning you and this call. The pastor can lead you accordingly. Jeremiah 3:15 says, “And I will give you pastors according to mine heart, which shall feed you with knowledge and understanding."

We are not saying that one person cannot possess more than one of these gifts, because they can. The anointed teacher can teach things that will help you grow in your walk and calling, things that will help you mature into the person God called you to be.

The evangelist can come along and energize or stir up the gift that is in you according to the leading of the Holy Ghost. All of these things work hand in hand so that the will of God may be done in the life of the called person. **Romans 8:28** says, "And we know that **all things work together for** good to them that love God, to them who are the called according to *his* purpose."

A good example is **James 5:14-15** which says "Is any sick among you? Let him call for the elders of the church; and let them pray over him, anointing him with oil in the name of the Lord: And the prayer of faith shall save the sick, and the Lord shall raise him up; and if he has committed sins, they shall be forgiven him."

In many cases, we do not discern or seek out who the elders in the church are, so that we may do according to the principles laid out in scripture. We call on those that we are comfortable with; those that we feel have like spirits, even if they are babes in Christ (church). We often wonder why things are not working the way they are supposed to. God is a God of order and principles. The way He laid things out, is the way He wants them carried out. He watches over His word to perform it.

Another thing we do sometimes is violate the principle found in Matthew 18:19, which says, "Again, I say unto you, that if two of you shall agree on earth as touching anything that they shall ask, it shall be done for them of my Father which is in heaven." This principle assures us that if two of us shall agree, whatever we ask shall be done for us by our Father which is in heaven. It is amazing to me how we sometimes ask people that we do not agree with, respect, or naturally get along with; to pray with us concerning specific things we believe the Lord for, yet we expect Him to do these things.

Amos 3:3 says "Can two walk together, except they be agreed"? We often say it this way, "How can two walk together except they be agreed (in agreement already). To be truly effective in changing our world, we must have a change in this pattern of practice.

CHAPTER TEN

LAUNCH INTO THE DEEP

I believe that there are deeper depths and higher heights we can reach in the wisdom and knowledge of Christ. Jesus told Peter in Luke 5:4 to launch out into the deep. To cast his net out into the deep and let it down for a catch. Peter was not a novice, this was his profession and he knew it very well. They had been out on the sea toiling all night and made no catch.

Jesus knew some things that Peter did not know. As we read on in the scripture, we see that it was not just any catch but a great and mighty catch. This came about after Simon (who is called Peter) humbled himself and surrendered his will to the will and word of Jesus. Given the character and temperament of Peter, this was a big change.

Psalms 42:7 talks about the deep call unto the deep. I want to tell you that Christ is the deep. Romans 10:7 say, "Who shall descend into the deep that is to bring Christ up from the dead." When we begin to diligently and earnestly seek

God's face not just His hand, we launch out into the deep things of God.

A few months ago as I was preparing for a speaking engagement, the Holy Spirit began to show me a revelation concerning seeking the Kingdom of God. In the vision, there were people traveling in an airplane or a car, and the pilot (or driver) made an announcement, "over there to your right is: The Kingdom of God." Everyone looked in amazement at the splendor of its beauty. They continued looking at it until it was out of site.

The Lord said this is how many of us view seeking the kingdom of God. We look at it, see it and later say, "I sought the kingdom of God." We did not do anything else with it. We did not stop to behold it or embrace it; we kept on going (seeking). The message here is, when we seek the kingdom of God, He (God) requires us to learn the rule and principles of God, to possess them and make them become a part of us so that we may operate in them. Jesus preached the kingdom; others preach the gospel of the kingdom. Jesus was able to preach the kingdom because He possessed the kingdom.

Likewise, many ministers and preachers today preach about the kingdom of God because it is the new "buzz word" everybody wants to know about. The problem is, just like the travelers in the vision, not many people possess the kingdom. Matthew 11:12 says, "And from the days of John the Baptist until now the kingdom of heaven suffereth violence, and the violent take it by force."

This scripture lets us know that possessing the kingdom is not going to be an easy walk through the park. It's going to take being relentless and militant spiritually to possess it. To possess something is to own it, have it in your possession, and have it become a part of you.

In Luke 17:20 the Pharisees demanded of Jesus to know when the kingdom of God would come. Jesus told them that the kingdom of God does not come with (by) observation. He went on to tell them that the kingdom of God is within you.

The apostle Paul said in 1 Corinthians 4:20, "The kingdom of God is not in word, but in power." Since the kingdom of God is not word or observation, it is power in you; this means when you possess the kingdom of God, wherever you go the kingdom goes with you.

Luke 12:32 says, "Fear not, little flock; for it is the Father's good pleasure to give you the kingdom." The design of God is, when people come in contact with you, they come in contact with the kingdom of God.

CHAPTER ELEVEN

CALL TO SERVICE

Recently the Holy Spirit impressed upon us to establish a prayer line, where anyone can call in at the appointed time and join us in prayer. Part of the instructions given to us was to make sure everyone on the line is saved or has been given the opportunity to accept Christ. The reason for this is so that we all would be on one accord. We all would be heirs of the promises and that we can pray in agreement (Amos 3:3).

One of the scriptures given to us was 1 John 5:14-15, which says, "This is the confidence we have in Him, that, if we ask anything according to His will, he hears us: And if we know that he hears us, whatsoever we ask, we know that we have the petitions that we desired of him."

The plan of God is for us to ask and pray according to His will that He may grant us our petition. I like the way Charles H. Spurgeon put it in the preface of the one-minute devotions "Faith's Checkbook," He says, "A promise from God may very instructively be compared to a check payable to order. It is given to the believer with the view of bestowing upon him some good thing. It is not meant that he should read it over comfortably, and then have done with it. No, he is to treat the promise as a reality, as a man treats a check."

Even after being in Christ and in the ministry for quite some time, my life completely changed when I realized I was an heir and joint heir with Christ. I knew this scripture and preached about it many times, but it wasn't until it resonated in my spirit that, everything changed for me. I began to see things differently and realized that all things are truly possible to them that believe.

The Holy Spirit began to open to me revelations about the scripture in Hosea 4:6 which says, "My people are destroyed for lack of knowledge: because thou hast rejected knowledge."

The Lord showed me a scenario of a man that was about to lose everything he had. He tried everything he could to keep it, but to no avail. One day after losing everything, he came across an old friend he had not seen in a long time. The old friend asked the man how he was doing since his long lost cousin died and left him a million dollars.

The man stood there in shock, and replied "What cousin?" "What million dollars?" The friend said, "You did not know your cousin left you a million dollars?" The man said "NO!"

The man stood there with thoughts going through his mind. He asked, “is this really true or is this some kind of joke?” The friend said, “all you have to do is go down to the courthouse and find out if it is true or not!” The man walked away thinking if it was even possible that this could be true. Then a glimmer of hope popped in his mind. All things are possible to them that believe.

He got to the courthouse, asked for the attorney of records, went to see the attorney and told the attorney the story. The attorney asked him for some identification and left to go check the records. He came back and said, "Yes sir, your cousin John passed away and left you a million dollars.” “Wow!" The man exclaimed, "Thank You Lord!" Then the man asked "What must I do to get the money?" The attorney said, "All you have to do is sign some documents to get the process started."

What the Lord showed me was, as soon as the man signed the documents, he was a legal millionaire! Even though he had not received one dime of the money, he still was a millionaire on paper.

The man stopped and paused in his excitement, and the thought came to his mind "Had I known this a few days ago, I could have saved my entire house and all." The moral of the story is; my people do perish because of the lack of knowledge. This means that everything that belongs to Christ, (Abraham) I have access to; I realized that all I have to do is change my culture and find out what I need to do to possess these things. This is God's message to you. Possess the kingdom. Everything we need is in the Kingdom, health and a cure, wholeness and wellness, deliverance from all sickness and diseases. If we can possess the Kingdom we can possess all these things and more.

The story of Elijah and Elisha

I want to draw your attention to a passage of scripture found in 2 Kings 2:9 where Elisha the prophet asked the prophet Elijah for a double portion of his spirit. In order to understand why he asked for this particular thing and how it all came about, we must go to 1Kings chapters 18 and 19. In chapter 19 of 1 Kings, we read that Elijah leaves his servants in Beersheba and flees from Jezebel.

And Ahab told Jezebel all that Elijah had done, and withal how he had slain all the prophets with the sword.

Then Jezebel sent a messenger unto Elijah, saying, so let the gods do to me, and more also, if I make not thy life as the life of one of them by to morrow about this time.

And when he saw that, he arose, and went for his life, and came to Beersheba, which belongeth to Judah, and left his servant there. 1 Kings 19:1-3

As we read on in verses 4-8 we see where Elijah desires to die because of fear of what Jezebel said she was going to do to him.

But he himself went a day's journey into the wilderness, and came and sat down under a juniper tree: and he requested for himself that he might die; and said, it is enough; now, O LORD, take away my life; for I am not better than my fathers.

And as he lay and slept under a juniper tree, behold, then an angel touched him, and said unto him, Arise and eat.

And he looked, and, behold, there was a cake baken on the coals, and a cruse of water at his head. And he did eat and drink, and laid him down again.

And the angel of the LORD came again the second time, and touched him, and said, Arise and eat; because the journey is too great for thee.

And he arose, and did eat and drink, and went in the strength of that meat forty days and forty nights unto Horeb the mount of God.

Something very interesting happened in verses 9-18, Elijah arrived at Mount Horeb (which is called the Mount of God) and lodged in a cave there. He began to have a pity party with himself, then the word of the Lord came to him and said to him, "What doest thy here, Elijah?"

Elijah began to explain that he had been very jealous for the Lord God of host: for the children of Israel had forsaken His covenant, thrown down His altars and slain His prophets with the sword and he alone is left and they seek his life, to take it away.

The scriptures do not say this, but I believe that after Elijah made his statement, the Lord decided to demonstrate something to Elijah that he would never forget. Take a look at the demonstration: "And he said, Go forth, and stand upon the mount before the LORD. And, behold, the LORD passed by, and a great and strong wind rent the mountains, and brake in pieces the rocks before the LORD; *but* the LORD *was* not in the wind: and after the wind an earthquake; *but* the LORD *was* not in the earthquake: And after the earthquake a fire; *but* the LORD *was* not in the fire: and after the fire a still small voice." (1 Kings 19:11-12).

After the Lord conducted the demonstration with Elijah, He asked him again, “what doest thou here Elijah?” Elijah was honest and told the Lord why he was there, he said "I have been very jealous for the LORD God of hosts: because the children of Israel have forsaken thy covenant, thrown down thine altars, and slain thy prophets with the sword; and I, *even* I only, am left; and they seek my life, to take it away." (1 Kings 19:14). This was the same answer Elijah gave the Lord the first time He asked.

I don't believe Elijah clearly understood the message the Lord was sending him. Surely the Lord knew why Elijah was there, but He wanted Elijah to understand something far greater than what was at hand. To grasp the point the Lord was making with Elijah, you would have to understand the show down that took place on Mount Carmel.

In chapter eighteen of 1 Kings starting at verse nineteen, we see that there was a showdown with Elijah, Ahab and the four hundred and fifty prophets of Baal. This showdown resulted in a victory for Elijah where he slew the four hundred and fifty prophets of Baal:

"Now therefore send, and gather to me all Israel unto Mount Carmel, and the prophets of Baal four hundred and fifty, and the prophets of the groves four hundred, which eat at Jezebel's table.

So Ahab sent unto all the children of Israel, and gathered the prophets together unto Mount Carmel. And Elijah came unto all the people, and said, how long halt ye between two opinions? If the LORD be God, follow him: but if Baal, then follow him. And the people answered him not a word.

Then said Elijah unto the people, I, even I only, remain a prophet of the LORD; but Baal's prophets are four hundred and fifty men.

Let t hem therefore give us two bullocks; and let them choose one bullock for themselves, and cut it in pieces, and lay it on wood, and put no fire under: and I will dress the other bullock, and lay it on wood, and put no fire under:

And call ye on the name of your gods, and I will call on the name of the LORD: and the God that answereth by fire, let him be God. And all the people answered and said, It is well spoken.

And Elijah said unto the prophets of Baal, Choose you one bullock for yourselves, and dress it first; for ye are many; and call on the name of your gods, but put no fire under.

And they took the bullock which was given them, and they dressed it, and called on the name of Baal from morning even until noon, saying, O Baal, hear us. But there was no voice, nor any that answered. And they leaped upon the altar which was made.

And it came to pass at noon, that Elijah mocked them, and said, Cry aloud: for he is a god; either he is talking, or he is pursuing, or he is in a journey, or peradventure he sleepeth, and must be awaked.

And they cried aloud, and cut themselves after their manner with knives and lancets, till the blood gushed out upon them. And it came to pass, when midday was past, and they prophesied until the time of the offering of the evening sacrifice, that there was neither voice, nor any to answer, nor any that regarded.

And Elijah said unto all the people, Come near unto me. And all the people came near unto him. And he repaired the altar of the LORD that was broken down.

And Elijah took twelve stones, according to the number of the tribes of the sons of Jacob, unto whom the word of the LORD came, saying, Israel shall be thy name: And with the stones he built an altar in the name of the LORD: and he made a trench about the altar, as great as would contain two measures of seed.

And he put the wood in order, and cut the bullock in pieces, and laid him on the wood, and said, Fill four barrels with water, and pour it on the burnt sacrifice, and on the wood.

And he said, Do it the second time. And they did it the second time. And he said, Do it the third time. And they did it the third time. And the water ran round about the altar; and he filled the trench also with water.

And it came to pass at the time of the offering of the evening sacrifice, that Elijah the prophet came near, and said, LORD God of Abraham, Isaac, and of Israel, let it be known this day that thou art God in Israel, and that I am thy servant, and that I have done all these things at thy word.

Hear me, O LORD, hear me, that this people may know that thou art the LORD God, and that thou hast turned their heart back again. Then the fire of the LORD fell, and consumed the burnt sacrifice, and the wood, and the stones, and the dust, and licked up the water that was in the trench.

And when all the people saw it, they fell on their faces: and they said, The LORD, he is the God; the LORD, he is the God.

And Elijah said unto them, Take the prophets of Baal; let not one of them escape. And they took them: and Elijah brought them down to the brook Kishon, and slew them there." (1 Kings 18:19-40)

Here we see the awesome power and demonstration of the true and living God. God poured out His Spirit upon one of His servants, and caused him to defeat four hundred and fifty prophets of another god. This gives credence to the scripture stated in Deuteronomy 32:30 "One can chase a thousand and two put ten thousand to flight."

This was a great victory for Elijah but the celebration of it was short lived. Shortly after this victory at Mount Carmel, it was told to Jezebel what happened there. Jezebel sent a message to Elijah that she was going to do to him what he did to her prophets. Elijah was afraid and decided to run and flee from her.

I believe this action of Elijah angered the Lord, prompting Him to ask Elijah (twice) why he was there under the tree. One important principle we all must realize and understand concerning God, is that: fear and faith cannot cohabitate together. Either we trust and believe in God or we don't. There is no middle ground.

Elijah's answer to God's question should have been anything other than, "I was afraid of Jezebel, so I ran." Surely, he did right by not lying to God, but that was not the right answer as far as God was concerned. God showed Elijah what the answer should have been through the demonstration of the wind, earthquake and fire.

What this demonstration said was "I am God. The God of all gods, beside Me there is no other." Who is Jezebel; or anyone else, that you should be mindful of or afraid of?

Because of Elijah's action and disposition, the Lord gave him another assignment to carry out. The Lord said to Elijah "Go, return on thy way to the wilderness of Damascus; when you get there anoint (appoint) Hazgel to be King over Syria, anoint Jehu to be King over Israel and anoint Elisha to be prophet in your place.

This signified that the Lord was changing leadership. He was bringing in a new regime of leaders that would trust Him and would not be afraid of anything or anyone. Look at what the Lord said about the new regime.

> "*And it shall come to pass, that him that escapeth the sword of Hazael shall Jehu slay: and him that escapeth from the sword of Jehu shall Elisha slay.*"
> *1 Kings 19:17*

The message the Lord was sending to Elijah, was the same message He gave to Joshua after He told Moses to appoint Joshua in his place. He said in **Joshua 1:5** "There shall not any man be able to stand before thee all the days of thy life: **as I was with Moses**, *so* I will be with thee: I will not fail thee, nor forsake thee."

God is saying to us that it is time to change our culture in order to change our world. It is time to move away from a culture of fear, doubt and skepticism about what God wants to say and do in this hour as well as who He want to use to do it. Doubt is unbelief in God and His word and therefore is sin. The scripture declares that no sin shall tarry in His sight, including doubt.

We must wrap ourselves in Psalms 23, and know that the Lord is our Shepherd and we shall not want for anything. We should also pay particular attention to verse four which says, "Yea though I walk through the valley of the shadow of death, I will fear no evil; for thy art with me, thy rod and thy staff shall comfort me." Verse six tells us;" Surely goodness and mercy shall follow us all the days of our life: and we will dwell in the house of the LORD forever."

In our world today, many of us are afraid to go deeper in the Lord mainly because of the old saying, "New levels mean new devils," so we opt to stay at the level we are at currently because, at least we know what we are dealing with. Although the old saying may be true to a degree, the principles of faith are still the same. If God kept you and brought you through at the current level, He will do the same thing at the new level. All He requires of us is to trust Him (have faith in Him) and believe that He is going to keep us at any level He calls us to. Just as Abraham judged Him faithful who called him.

All things are possible to him that believes. To understand 2 Kings 2:9 you must understand that it was no coincidence that Elisha asked for a double portion as some would have you believe. In Amos 3:7 it says, "Surely the Lord God will do nothing, but He reveals His secret to His servants, the Prophets." This is proven in Genesis 18:17 where God said, "Shall I hide from Abraham that thing which I do?"

The word of the Lord had already gone out in 1 Kings... where the Lord told Elijah to anoint Elisha to be prophet in His stead/place and Elisha knew this. How did he know this? (1) By the Spirit as a Prophet and (2) other Prophets told this to Elisha, and he said he already knew of it. This set the stage for the fulfillment of the scripture "All things are possible to him that believes." (Mark 9:23)

When Elisha realized, God not only called him to be a Prophet, but to take the place of Elijah the Prophet, who was one of the greatest Prophets of the time. Elisha thought, what an opportunity to be blessed and highly favored of the Lord, to not only wear his anointing but also to have the anointing of this great man of God. Wow, what a privilege and honor this would be.

This is where the idea of a double portion came from. The story is told in 2 Kings 2:9, where the Prophet Elijah said to Elisha, "Ask what shall I do for thee, before I be taken away from thee?" Out of all the things Elisha could have asked for, he asked for a double portion, not of the Holy Spirit but a double portion of Elijah's spirit. Elijah replied "you asked a hard thing."

One reason it was a hard thing was this was the first time anyone had ever asked this of him or anyone else, for that matter. After pondering this request for a moment, Elijah said, "nevertheless (I tell you what), if you see me when I leave you can have the double portion, if you don't see me leave, it won't happen. Now the conditions were set to make this possibility a reality. All Elisha has to do is see Elijah leave and it would be a done deal, he could have his request.

The scriptures says in verse eleven of the same chapter "And it came to pass, as they went on and talked (walking and talking) behold, there appeared a chariot of fire, and horses of fire and parted them both assunder, and Elijah went up by a whirlwind into heaven."

The next verse says "And Elisha **saw it** and he cried, My Father, my father (look, look I see it), the chariot of Israel and the horsemen thereof, and he saw him no more." We would like to point out what happened next after Elisha saw Elijah taken away in the whirlwind.

The scripture says, "And Elisha took a hold of his own clothes and tore them in two pieces, and took up (put on) the mantle that fell from Elijah." Elisha **immediately** began to **function** in the double portion anointing of Elijah (see verses 14-25). He did not wait for nor did he go looking for a confirmation from another Prophet, King, Apostle or anyone else. He knew himself that he had met the terms and conditions set forth for him to receive the double portion.

This was a change of culture for Elisha; he went from operating in his anointing to operating in the double portion Elijah gave him. This not only changed Elisha's world, but also the world of the people around him.

Notes of understanding: Who was Baal? The word Baal means, lord, possessor, husband. Baal was the name of the supreme god worshiped in ancient Canaan and Phoenicia. The practice of Baal worship infiltrated Jewish religious life during the time of the Judges, Judges 3:7, it became widespread in Israel during the reign of Ahab (1 Kings 16:31-33) and also affected Judah (2 Chronicles 28:1-2). The word *baal* means "lord"; the plural is *Baalim*. In general, Baal was a fertility god who was believed to enable the earth to produce crops and people to produce children.

Different regions worshiped Baal in different ways, and Baal proved to be a highly adaptable god. Various locales emphasized one or another of his attributes and developed special "denominations" of Baalism. Baal of Peor (Numbers 25:3) and Baal-Berith (Judges 8:33) are two examples of such localized deities.

Who was Jezebel? Jezebel's story is found in 1 and 2 Kings. She was the daughter of Ethbaal, king of Tyre/Sidon and priest of the cult of Baal, a cruel, sensuous and revolting false god whose worship involved sexual degradation and lewdness. Ahab, king of Israel, married Jezebel and led the nation into Baal worship (1 Kings 16:31). Ahab and Jezebel's reign over Israel is one of the saddest chapters in the history of God's people.

ADOPTION

CHOSEN BY THE FATHER

Blessed be the God and Father of our Lord Jesus Christ, whom has blessed us with all spiritual blessings (gifts) in heavenly places in Christ. According as He has chosen us in Him before the foundation of the world, that we should be holy and without blame before Him in love; having predestinated us into the adoption of children by Jesus Christ to Himself, according to the good pleasure of His will. To the praise of the glory of His grace, wherein He hath made us accepted in the beloved. (Ephesians 1:3-6 KJV).

I believe it is very important that we bring clarity and understanding to this particular subject which is at the heart of the Father. Adoption to God is much more than just a thought of something that takes place in the course of our lives. The

Bible describes adoption as the legal act of **investing in (with) son ship.**

When children are adopted in the natural, they take on the name, culture and personification of the adopting parent. They become the responsibility of the adopting parent. The same thing happens with the kingdom of God.

We are adopted of the Beloved into the kingdom of God through Jesus Christ our Lord. He becomes responsible for us and our well-being. We have His promise on this in Philippians 4:19 which says, "My God shall supply all of my needs according to His riches in glory."

David, the chief Psalmist tells us in the 23 Psalm that the Lord is our shepherd and we shall not want. He says that the good shepherd makes us to lie down in green pastures. He causes us to rest in a place of plenty where there is no lack. He restores our souls.

When the Lord restores our soul, He doesn't just refresh us, He makes us better than new. You may ask how anyone can be made better than new. Well, first of all, with God, all things are possible.

Second, we were born in sin and shaped in iniquity. When the Lord restores us, He renews us to Him and adds to us all that which was lost and more, so that we may redeem the time.

Psalms 84:11 says, "For the LORD God *is* a sun and shield: the LORD will give grace and glory: no good *thing* will he **withhold** from them that walk uprightly."

The Apostle Paul declares in **1 Corinthians 2:9**, "But as it is written, Eye hath not seen, nor ear heard, neither have entered into the heart of man, the things which God hath prepared for them that love him." The Apostle Paul goes on to say in verse 10, "But God hath revealed *them* unto us by his Spirit: for the Spirit searcheth all things, yea, the deep things of God."

A few years ago, the Lord revealed to us through the Holy Spirit that all of this is about to change. This is what He said to us: "You know how you all say, eyes have not seen, ears have not heard..." I said, "Yes Lord." He said, "well, eyes are about to see and ears are about to hear what I'm about to do." This is truly amazing because we are living in a time when nothing less than His good, perfect, and manifested Will, will do.

When the Lord gave us the assignment to do this writing, He began to reveal to us many things concerning His Kingdom and its Culture. One of those things is found in **Matthew 12:25** which says, "And Jesus knew their thoughts, and said unto them, every kingdom divided against itself is brought to desolation; and every city or **house divided** against itself shall not stand."

For everyone that names the name of the Lord and is a part of His kingdom, the Lord would have us to know that there should be no breakdown in communication between us, because we all have this one thing in common (Acts 2), we all have been grafted in (adopted) and accepted of the Beloved. We all have the same Father and are a part of the same Kingdom, the Kingdom of God.

There is no difference between the Jews and the Greeks (Romans 10:12), the Africans and the Asians, the Americans and the Australian's etc. There should be no racial, ethnic and cultural difference between us. Jesus said in the book of John, Me and My Father are one. He prayed to the

Father to make them (you and I and those that are called by His name) one as you and I are one (John 17:21-22). This should be our prayer also.

1 Corinthians 12:25 says, "That there should be no schism in the body; but *that* the members should have the same care one for another." If there be any indifference between us, it means that we have not been made perfect by love (John 17: 23, 1 John4:18). Usually, the reason for indifference is a spirit of fear.

It is not necessarily the fear of being afraid of one another, but the feeling of inferiority or short coming in one's own life. Also because of not knowing from where they came, and that they are not of the same fold. We begin to justify ourselves.

What happens in many cases is, when we come into the kingdom of God, we bring whatever our social and cultural background is, into the kingdom, not realizing that these things are not supposed to come into the kingdom with us. This is why the Lord is saying in this hour, "Change your culture, Change your world."

You may have been brought up in a part of the world where it is part of your culture to hate or dislike a certain group or groups of people. To you, these groups of people are viewed as your enemies. When you come into the kingdom of God, this changes because one of the rules of the kingdom of God is to love your enemies and pray for them. When we come in Christ, we become new creatures. We take on the cultural attributes and identity of kingdom citizens, subjected to the King and His rule. In a kingdom, the word of the king is law. No debate, no democracy.

CHAPTER TWELVE

WAITING ON THE WORLD TO CHANGE

I was asked to speak at an event held at the Cultural Center in our city and the theme of the event was "Change." This event was sponsored by Apostle Albert and Linda Delone of "To the Glory of God Ministries" with Pastor Rachael Harrison serving as the MC. Usually when I am asked to minister somewhere my first response is, let me pray about it and get back with you. This time was different. I felt in my spirit to accept the invitation immediately but I began to ask the Lord why I accepted the invitation without consulting Him like I normally do, consult Him first. I said, Lord I'm concerned about this.

The Lord reminded me that He had been dealing with me and speaking with me concerning this subject and this book for over a year now. Even though we teach and believe there are no coincidences or happenstances with the Lord, everything is by divine appointment; I still thought "how ironic it is" to be asked to speak at an event at the "Culture Center" about this particular subject "Change."

The next day as I was thinking about this, I thought it would be a good idea to take the day off and go to the gym, and start studying/seeking the Lord concerning the message the following day, since the event is about two weeks away. How wrong was I? When I got to the gym and was preparing for my workout, the Lord began to speak to me about the message I was to deliver at the event.

He said this is your message. I kind of chuckled and said within myself, "Lord, I haven't started seeking you yet for the message," but at the same time I knew that I had better follow the leading of the Lord and not quench the Holy Ghost. So I did as the Lord instructed me. He began to give me the entire message to deliver at the event.

I began to hear a song in my mind that I could not remember where or when I heard the song. So I asked my children if they knew of a song with these words in it. They pulled up a song and played it. I said, that's the song I've been hearing!

The song had a nice beat to it and the words said, "WAITING ON THE WORLD TO CHANGE."

I said Lord I found the song. What is it you are saying concerning this song and message? The Lord said this is the position most people take, they are waiting on the world to change to determine what they are going to do. He said this is not my will or my plan for their lives. The message is this; while we are waiting on the world to change, God is waiting on us to change so that we may effect a change upon the world.

If you search the Bible you will see that God has always used the remnant or a small few to accomplish His will and to bring about a change on the entire world. When I think about the story of Noah and the Ark, out of all the people in the world at that time, only eight people (and the animals) entered the Ark to start a new world. When God decided to destroy Sodom and Gomorrah, there were only a few people saved, Abraham, his nephew Lot, their wives, children and servants.

We cannot leave out Rahab, the harlot. Hebrews 11:31 says, "By faith the harlot Rahab perished not with them that believed not, when she had received the spies with peace." You can read about Rahab and her story in Joshua chapter two, chapter six and James 2:25 this is an amazing story that will inspire you.

Even Jesus in the New Testament took twelve disciples, poured Himself in to them, made them apostles and commissioned them to go into all the world and make disciples. God is waiting for us to change, to turn to Him whole heartily and let Him lead the way for us. He declared in His word that He is the way, the truth and the life; no man can come unto the Father except through Him.

In the message for the event, the Lord showed me the scripture in Matthew 3:1-2 that says "In those days came John the Baptist, preaching in the wilderness of Judaea, And saying, Repent ye: for the kingdom of heaven is at hand." As we mentioned earlier, the word repent means to change, change direction. He said to me, John the Baptist went through the wilderness of Judaea saying repent for the kingdom of Heaven is a hand, here is a person going through the city (our city) saying "Change, for the Kingdom of Heaven is at hand."

The Lord began to say, this was the same thing John the Baptist did. Although John the Baptist used the word repent and you are using the word change, they mean the same thing with the same expected results. I said, Lord, how so? He showed me the scripture in Mark chapter two.

In this chapter, Jesus entered into the town of Capernaum and it was told to the people of that town that Jesus was in the house and immediately many were gathered together, so much that there was not enough room to hold them all as Jesus preached the word to them. Someone tore the roof of the house open and let down, on a stretcher, a person sick of the Palsy.

When Jesus saw their faith, He said to the person sick of the Palsy "Son, thy sins be forgiven thee." Some of the scribes sitting there reasoning in their hearts, "Why does this man speak blasphemies? Who can forgive sins but God only?" When Jesus perceived in His Spirit that they reasoned within themselves, He said unto them, "Why reason ye these things in your hearts? Whether is it easier to say to the sick of the Palsy, thy sins be forgiven thee; or to say Arise, and take up thy bed and walk?"

What Jesus was saying was, it does not matter which way or which one of these things I say, they both mean the same thing. They both will yield the same results. This is what Jesus is saying to us today concerning "Change your Culture, Change your World." He is saying repent from your old ways of and change to the ways that represent "Kingdom Culture."

The Lord went on to say, "In your message, spell out the word change like this:"

C **C**harge them

H **H**im/her

A **A**nd everyone there

N **N**ot to remain the same, but change. Charge them to

G **G**ive this message to

E **E**veryone they come in contact with.

It was a beautiful message we shared with the people at the event that evening. Now we are sharing this message with you, we pray that you will accept this message and share it with everyone you come in contact with.

SIDE NOTE: Concerning sin and sickness from Mark chapter two. Several years ago, I set my face like a flint to seek God in prayer and fasting concerning what appeared to be a lot of sickness going on all around the country, especially among the body of Christ and the people that were in church. I said "Lord, I don't understand what is going on; everywhere you look people are sick with something?" The Lord's response was quick, simple and profound as if He had been waiting on someone to ask Him what was going on. He said "Get the sin out, the sickness will leave." My response was "What!" I surely don't understand this.

The Lord repeated it again "Get the sin out and the sickness will leave." I said Lord; I know there are people that do not smoke, drink, chew, commit adultery or any of these things, yet they are going through just as the others. He said "that may be true, but did you know that doubt and unbelief is sin? Did you know that to know to do good and not do it is sin also?"

The point here is; it is not solely about the things that others can see, it is also those hidden things that only the Holy Spirit can see and discern that can stand in the way and hinder us from obtaining our healing. Here is a very interesting thought. 1 Samuel 15:25 KJV says, "Rebellion is as the sin of witchcraft." In other words, rebellion is the same sin as witchcraft. When we look at the words rebellion and witchcraft, it changes the scope of things.

Do you know how many people walk in rebellion and may not realize it because they are not clear about what rebellion really is? Did you know that there are people from different backgrounds, groups and walks of life that deal with witchcraft? Did you also know that many of these people are in our churches? Did you know that God views witchcraft as sin and has a plan to deal with it?

CHAPTER THIRTEEN

NIC AT NIGHT

No, this is not the famous cartoon network we see on TV. This is about a real person that lived on the earth more than two thousand years ago. This person had the same position and mindset that many of us have today. In the Bible this person is known as Nicodemus who went to Jesus at night to inquire of Him about His teachings on being born again. His story can be found in St. John chapter three.

Nicodemus was not just an ordinary man. He was a Pharisee and a ruler of the Jews. He was a member of the Sanhedrin Court which was the Supreme Court of ancient Israel that was made up of 71 members. He interviewed Christ at Jerusalem and was taught by Christ the doctrine of the New Birth which can be found in St. John 3:1-15. Nicodemus defended Christ before the Sanhedrin court (St. John 7:50-52) and assisted at His burial (St. John 19:39-42).

He came to Jesus by night because he did not want to offend his fellow members of the

Sanhedrin court and he did not understand Jesus teachings about being born again.

Jesus proclaimed to Nicodemus the need for spiritual regeneration and He condemned him for his spiritual blindness because he professed to be a teacher of spiritual things but could not see what Jesus meant about being born again.

Here we have a picture of a person that, to our knowledge did not participate in any of the things that we know that would keep one from entering the kingdom of God, and was well versed in the scriptures and the laws of the word of God. Yet there was one thing missing, he was not born again. Jesus declared to him that one must be born again in order to enter the kingdom of God.

We are living in a time where information and knowledge is at our finger tips and can be easily accessed. Jesus is letting us know that it is not about our knowledge or our intellect that He is searching for. He is looking for disciples that have been truly born again, born of the Spirit and the water that He may reveal Himself to. Jesus said Himself that it is given to the disciples to know the mysteries of the kingdom of God and heaven.

Those that are outside of the Kingdom of God cannot understand the things concerning the Kingdom of God. No matter how much they read; study or attend churches, Seminaries and universities. The natural person (intellect) cannot grasp or understand the things of the Spirit because they are spiritually discerned. This is the standard God put in place for all of mankind.

Apparently, Nicodemus accepted Christ's teachings and became born again. This is evident by Nicodemus defending Christ when the Sanhedrin was enraged against Christ, John 7:37-38. Nicodemus also gave evidence in favor of Christ at the trial before Pilate, in which he was deprived of his office and banished from Jerusalem by the hostile Jews.

He made a public profession of his faith in Christ and that he was a follower of Christ at Christ's burial. He took his own personal wealth and purchased the mixture of myrrh and aloes that were used to embalm the body of Christ.

CONCLUSION

I believe that we can safely conclude that in order to change our world; we have to make some changes in the way we do things. This includes our mindsets, habits and hang-up's. In order to see Matthew 6:10 ("Thy will be done in earth, as it is in heaven") manifested in our lives, there must also be a change in our policies, plans and purposes at every level, locally, nationally and globally.

No, it is not too late, neither are we too far gone to make a change in our world. The Prophet Isaiah declared that it was in the year that King Uzziah died that everything changed for him. He said that was the year He saw the Lord high and lifted up. His train filled the temple. (Isaiah 6:1)

It was the year the King died that Isaiah was commissioned by the Lord to be a prophet. The seraphims that Isaiah saw functioned as God's agents in commissioning Isaiah. Isaiah could understand them when they spoke to him and when they praised God. Isaiah was called at a time when moral and spiritual laxity had reached its peak. Although, King Uzziah was a relatively good king and his reign was long and prosperous, many of his people turned away from God.

The prophet Isaiah made a very important discovery and confession when he saw the Lord. He said, "Woe is me! For I am undone; because I am a man of unclean lips, and I dwell in the midst of a people of unclean lips: for mine eyes have seen the King, the Lord of hosts." (Isaiah 6:5)

Isaiah confessed to the Lord that he didn't know it all; neither did he have it all together. In fact, "I have a dirty mouth," he said. Isaiah saw that this was just a small problem because one of the seraphims flew over to him with a hot coal and touched his mouth and lips, declaring that his iniquity was taken away and his sins purged. The big problem Isaiah faced was the fact that he lived with a people of unclean lips. Even after being delivered and cleansed from this, he had to go home and be exposed to this all over again. Isaiah realized he had to change his culture.

The Prophet Habakkuk had a similar problem to that of the prophet Isaiah. Habakkuk had a heavy burden and was saddened by the corruption he saw around him. He poured out his heart to God and said, "O Lord, how long shall I cry, and thou will not hear! Even cry out unto thee of violence, and thou will not save! Why dost thou show me iniquity, and cause me to behold grievance, for spoiling and violence are before me: and there are that raise up strife and contention. Therefore the law is slacked, and judgment doth never go forth: for the wicked doth compass about the righteous; therefore wrong judgment proceedeth." (Habakkuk 1:2-4)

God responds to Habakkuk's questions and concerns by saying, "Behold ye among the heathen, and regard, and wonder marvelously: for I will work a work in your days, which ye will not believe, though it be told you."

Notice how God responded. Behold ye among the heathen, (an unconverted people that do not acknowledge the God of the Bible). God was saying to the prophet although they do not believe, just watch and see. I'm going to do some amazing things even though they see it they still won't believe it. These things will not go unpunished. No matter how the circumstances may look, we must make a change in our culture in order to change our world.

Perhaps the late great King of Pop, Michael Jackson said it best in his hit song "Man in the mirror." He said, "If you want to make a change in the world, you must start with the man in the mirror."

"Gotta make a change
For once in my life
It's gonna feel real good
Gonna make a difference
Gonna make it right

I'm starting with the man in the mirror
I'm asking him to change his ways
And no message could have been any clearer
If you wanna make the world a better place
Take a look at yourself and then make a change"

NOTES OF UNDERSTANDING

The Old Testament: We know that the Old Testament was considered as a type and shadow of things to come, paving the way for future history. The showdown at Mount Carmel should settle any arguments anyone has concerning having other gods. There is only one true and living God; He is the Lord God Almighty. It should not matter if we believe this or accept this, it is a proven and established fact, according to scripture, that there is only one true and living God, and His name is Yahweh/ Jehovah God.

Abraham was not a religion. He was a real person that was given a real covenant promise by God that is still in effect today. As seeds of Abraham, in order for us to inherit the promises given to Abraham, we must meet the criteria and qualifications, one of which is, being in Christ.

Jesus (The Christ) is not a religion. He is a real person that was sent to the earth by God the Father through the virgin birth (Immaculate Conception). He lived, suffered and died a horrible death. He was buried in a borrowed tomb and was raised from the dead on the third day.

He is now seated at the right hand of the Father (God) making intercession for us (you and I). The problem we have today is, too many are in religion and not in Christ. In many parts of the world, it is the culture of the people to be in church and to be a part of some religion. This is why the heart of God is crying out to the people of the world to Change their Culture. Do not be in religion, be in Christ. Jesus did not come into the world to give us religion. He came that we may have eternal life through Him. He is the author of Eternal Life.

REFERENCES

PREFACE: "A Change Gonna Come" Sam Cooke, Wikipedia, the Free Encyclopedia.

Apostle Vincent G. Valentyn PhD, Kingdom Lifestyle Ministries, Cape Town South Africa and Harvey, La (USA)

Dale Carnegie: The Quick And Easy Way To Effective Speaking, Dale Carnegie and Associates, INC. 1992

INTRODUCTION: The Spiritual Man, Watchman Nee, Christian Literature Crusade (June 1, 1968)

Matters of the heart, Prophetess Juanita Bynum, Charisma House (Oct 2002)

Chapter One: Culture Defined, Merriam-Webster Dictionary

Chapter One: Dr. Don Colbert M. D. Fasting Made Easy, Published by Siloam 2004

Traditions: Wikipedia, the Free Encyclopedia

Chapter Two: Definitions, Dictionary.com

Chapters Six and Seven: Holy Martyr Photini of Samaria; Saints to Sisterhood, The lives of forty-eight Holy Women, Light &Life Publication Company. Other sources: **www.oca.org**, www.catholic.com

Chapter Eleven: Charles H. Spurgeon, One Minute Devotion, Faith Check Book

Chapter Twelve: Apostle Albert Delone, Prophetess Linda Delone, To The Glory Of God Ministries, New Orleans, La

Prophetess Rachael Harrison: God's Helping Hands Ministries, New Orleans, La

Chapter Thirteen: Nick at Night, Nicodemus, Orr, James, M,A,DD, General Editor "Definition", for Nicodemus; Bible History .com

Conclusion: Man in the Mirror by Michael Jackson. Written by, Siedah Garrett and Glen Ballard. Produced by, Quincy Jones. Information, **www.songfacts.com**

Index Page: 49 General Commands of Christ; **billgothard.com**

INDEX PAGE

49 General Commands of Christ

What are 49 Ways to Love God and Others?

The theme of all Scripture is to love God with all of our hearts and to love one another, Matthew 22:40 and John 13:34.

Repent—Matthew 4:17—Humility

Follow Me—Matthew 4:19—Meekness

Rejoice—Matthew 5:12—Joyfulness

Let Your Light Shine—Matthew 5:16—Generosity

Honor God's Law—Matthew 5:17–18—Love

Be Reconciled—Matthew 5:24–25—Responsibility

Do Not Commit Adultery—Matthew 5:29–30—Self-Control

Keep Your Word—Matthew 5:37—Truthfulness

Go the Second Mile—Matthew 5:38–42—Deference

Love Your Enemies—Matthew 5:44—Creativity

Be Perfect—Matthew 5:48—Sincerity

Practice Secret Disciplines—Matthew 6:1–18—Faith

Lay Up Treasures—Matthew 6:19–21—Thriftiness

Seek God's Kingdom—Matthew 6:33—Initiative

Judge Not—Matthew 7:1—Discernment

Do Not Cast Pearls—Matthew 7:6—Discretion

Ask, Seek, and Knock—Matthew 7:7–8—Resourcefulness

Do Unto Others—Matthew 7:12—Sensitivity

Choose the Narrow Way—Matthew 7:13–14—Decisiveness

Beware of False Prophets—Matthew 7:15—Alertness

Pray For Laborers—Matthew 9:38—Compassion

Be Wise as Serpents—Matthew 10:16—Wisdom

Fear God, Not Man—Matthew 10:26—Boldness

Hear God's Voice—Matthew 11:15—Attentiveness

Take My Yoke—Matthew 11:29—Obedience

Honor Your Parents—Matthew 15:4—Honor/Reverence

Beware of Leaven—Matthew 16:6—Virtue

Deny Yourself—Luke 9:23—Determination

Despise Not Little Ones—Matthew 18:10—Tolerance

Go to Offenders—Matthew 18:15—Justice

Beware of Covetousness—Luke 12:15—Contentment

Forgive Offenders—Matthew 18:21–22—Forgiveness

Honor Marriage—Matthew 19:6—Loyalty

Be a Servant—Matthew 20:26–28—Availability

Be a House of Prayer—Matthew 21:13—Persuasiveness

Ask in Faith—Matthew 21:21–22—Patience

Bring in the Poor—Luke 14:12–14—Hospitality

Render to Caesar—Matthew 22:19–21—Gratefulness

Love the Lord—Matthew 22:37–38—Enthusiasm

Love Your Neighbor—Matthew 22:39—Gentleness

Await My Return—Matthew 24:42–44—Punctuality

Take, Eat, and Drink—Matthew 26:26–27—Thoroughness

Be Born Again—John 3:7—Security

Keep My Commandments—John 14:15—Diligence

Watch and Pray—Matthew 26:41—Endurance

Feed My Sheep—John 21:15–16—Dependability

Baptize My Disciples—Matthew 28:19—Cautiousness

Receive God's Power—Luke 24:49—Orderliness

Make Disciples—Matthew 28:20—Flexibility

OTHER PRODUCTS BY APOSTLES TIMOTHY & PAMELA WILLIAMS

LET THE RIVERS FLOW, GOD'S WORD REVEALED

CONCERNING TITHES AND OFFERINGS

ISBN 0595367704

Book Description

Publication Date: **November 7, 2005**

Let the Rivers Flow is an easy to read, easy to understand guide to God's financial plan for His people. It is suitable for all ages and all walks of life. In order to maximize your blessing and potential blessings, you must have an understanding of the vehicles and how to properly use the tools to maximize your blessing potential.

To tithe or not to tithe? If tithe, then who, when. where, what, and why? What are the differences between tithes and offerings? What is the will of God concerning these subjects? Who has known the mind of the Lord concerning these matters? These and many other questions will be answered as you read and meditate on this book *Let the Rivers Flow*.

"This book *Let the Rivers Flow* by Apostles Timothy and Pamela Williams, gives us facts, figures, and many scriptures straight from God's word. It provides us with the knowledge we need concerning the wonderful experience of giving."—Gertrude Kelly, Hope Well Missionary Baptist Church, Norcross, GA

"The book *Let the Rivers Flow* by Apostles Tim and Pam Williams is very timely and very much needed. I found its teaching and instructions to be clear, precise, thorough and easy to read. Anyone after reading this book should be able to get the revelation of the importance of obeying God's command to bring all the tithes into the storehouse."—Antoinette Derrickson, Life in Christ Cathedral, PA

Touch N Lives Around The World LLC
ISBN-13: 978-0985413217
ISBN-10: 0985413212

List Price: **$12.99**

"Kingdom Power and Authority" transcends gender and denominations to bring a clear message of what true Power and Authority really means.
Power, everybody wants it; Politicians, School Administrators,
Corporate Executives right on down to the newest dealer on the street.
Everyone wants to wield the power but not many are willing to yield to
the power. In one place, on one stage, Dr. Emmanuel and his wife bring
together two of the most powerful concepts known to mankind, Power and
Authority. Revealing; 1. The Origin of Power and Authority. 2. Who has
it? 3. What does it means for us today?

www.createspace.com/3924588

ABOUT THE AUTHORS

Timothy and Pamela Williams are called by the will of God to be apostles to equip, edify, and perfect the Body of Christ with the mission of "Returning the Heart of Man back to God." They also have a mandate to prepare the Body of Christ for His return. They have more than twenty-five years in ministry and a strong anointing to encourage every individual to take their rightful place in the body of Christ and to be all that God called them to be.

www.ingramcontent.com/pod-product-compliance
Lightning Source LLC
LaVergne TN
LVHW020627100826
845148LV00012B/2082